A Spiritual Guide to Sabbath Economics

MAKING LOVE WITH MONEY

JUDITH L. FAVOR

Cover Photo by Esther Elizabeth

Wasteland Press
Shelbyville, KY USA
www.wastelandpress.net

A Spiritual Guide to Sabbath Economics: Making Love with Money
by Judith L. Favor

First Printing—November 2008
ISBN: 978-1-60047-253-4
Cover Photo by Esther Elizabeth

Printed in the U.S.A.

CONTENTS

FOREWORD

Engaging in a process of discernment regarding love (sex) and money may, to a naïve reader, seem like touching a third rail in politics. Relationships blossom and wither. Conversations flourish or are silenced. A common language is difficult to attain when the reader must absorb definitions and contexts, wending her/his way through a thicket of questions. Judith Favor addresses questing souls for whom the restlessness and anomie of contemporary culture has compromised meaning and purpose. A welter of beliefs and philosophies abound in today's multi-cultural context, a plethora of faith choices parallel to those of our consumerist society.

The American economy depends upon consumerism, buying and selling; most of us can scarcely fathom an economic system not based on laissez faire capitalism. But since October, 2008, any underlying trust that one might have in the monetary system or global capitalism has been undermined by financial meltdowns in the United States. As of this writing, institutions like Fannie Mae and Freddie Mac, AIG, Lehman Brothers, Merrill Lynch, Wachovia Bank and others are teetering.

A book like this, appearing during a time of economic uncertainty and lengthening recession, is asking questions that you, the reader, might really rather not ask. What is my relationship to money and how does that affect my relationship with the significant people in my life? Is my "love of money" so deeply engrained in my pursuit of the good life that I cannot step back from my current fear and see how the crisis that Americans are experiencing is not merely financial but deeply spiritual?

Taking a giant stride from the bills on the kitchen table to the deeply introspective and centering life of prayer and meditation is not crying out to Providence to save us from our greed and mistaken choices. Instead it is nothing less than a reclamation (transformation) of the totality of life lived under God (as our money declares on its face), a reclamation that is the work of a lifetime. This book hopes such reclamation can be reflectively pursued both by individual questioning and by asking hard questions in a community context. None of us can arrive at a meaningful life alone. One of the most important choices an individual makes is the community whose values she/he embraces and whose members form a supportive fellowship for discernment and action. So the first task of the naïve reader is to identify one's primary community and to piece the ideas in this book into one's experience of that community. These fragments of thought and action may remain fragmented, as do most of our lives, but for the writer, who is avowedly Christian, the spiritual life needs to be grounded in community.

A second task of the reader is to be patient when encountering vocabulary that can only deepen through experience. It owes much not only to scriptures of the Jewish and Christian traditions but also to elements of ecological thinking—earth, air, fire and water. The author revisions God in multiple images such as Light, Mystery, Source of Life, the Ultimate, Holy Spirit, Energy, Wisdom, etc. For those who are new to spiritual formation and wondering how to begin, pay particular attention to some "how to's" of prayer and meditation in Chapter Ten. Also give particular attention in Chapter Three to Ched Myer's summary in which the Sabbath Economics process is described as personal and communal, active and receptive.

Not everyone may resonate with the term Sabbath, the rest God affords after days of creation, but most people familiar with the busyness of life will understand the need for "time out," a change of pace for stress relief. Sabbath, however, has a far deeper context here, an integration of "rest" into all aspects of life, including love (sex) and money.

To help others along the path to such integration the writer tells her own story of love and money and includes the experiences of a variety of women and men. Recalling the economic history of one's own family and the complex relationships it entails may not be a familiar exercise, but it is a prerequisite to understanding the power and promise that love and money offers. Depending upon the generation of the reader, one may recall The Great Depression, World War II, the war's aftermath of prosperity, the guns and butter era of the 1960s including the War on Poverty, the booms and the busts of succeeding decades, the government denigration beginning in the Reagan era, the prosperity of the 1990s and the profligate spending of the 2000s. Whether the current prospect of living with less is unsettling to you depends upon your family's economic situation, the attitudes toward money you have absorbed and whether your faith perspective calls you to a generosity beyond your present imagining.

Your spiritual perspective may not be without challenge or conflict as it deepens in response to the questing of this book. You may find yourself tentatively moving toward actions you had not previously entertained or positions that distance you from many you care about. The spiritual journey has always been thus. The author cannot proscribe nor even describe what your journey might be. But she affirms that the journey is possible. Perhaps that is enough.

Elsie Harber, Claremont, California
October, 2008

CHAPTER ONE:
INTRODUCTION: A SPIRITUAL GUIDE

LIFE HAPPENS

Change is an ever-present reality. Each of us meets change
with love and money in exceedingly different ways.
                                                    Judith Favor

Unwelcome change comes in all shapes and sizes—from massive, public and catastrophic to small, private and subtle. When good stuff happens we enjoy the illusion of having it all together. When things fall apart we feel challenged to find new ways of re-establishing balance, or at least predictability. Any sort of change offers opportunity for spiritual guidance when trouble leaves us willing move beyond the current comfort zone. Love and money contain all the conflicts and growth opportunities that anyone needs to grow spiritually. John Shea summarizes it well: *All our devices to make life safe—amassing money and military might—are ultimately only stalls. Our meanings are fragile, our loves passing, our hopes precarious. When the reliability of all we have constructed is brought into question, we enter the dimension of Mystery."*

SPIRITUAL GUIDANCE

Who will care about our entanglements with the Ultimate?
                                                    Carolyn Gratton

Mystery can be terrifying territory. Experienced spiritual guides may know the terrain. A good guide can help us to find new ground for confused minds, troubles hearts or aching bodies. This guide offers some assistance but cannot take the place of a trusting relationship with a skilled companion, someone who knows you, loves you, and walks with you through the valley of the shadow of doubt. Touching holy ground is very different from getting on top of things. The art of spiritual guidance leads toward the realm of The Really Real and it goes way beyond psychological coping techniques.

Most people—the author included—look for some kind of guidance when life gets overwhelming. Confusion, debt, pain, loss—even startling moments of wonder—jolt women and men into search-mode. Where can we find a source of wisdom to lead us into connection with larger purpose and meaning? This guide invites you to search within for spiritual wisdom by wrestling with both the messiness and the mystery of money. Be still, says the Psalmist, and know God.

When life gives us a nasty jolt, it is natural for humans to pray. HELP! as the first and most gut-wrenching appeal to a source larger than my little self. If the jolt is awesome the prayer tends be WOW! or THANKS! When hard change happens it points us in new directions. Who will help us let go of patterns that block us from participation in a fuller life? Spiritual guides honor the messy stuff that happens while also inviting us to look at life in a larger perspective. We, the people, tend to defend against change and growth through endlessly inventive forms of evading The Holy. Loss of partner, parent or child, loss of work, loss of self-image, even loss of a favorite concept can open us to formative changes. When unwelcome hits with love and money come your way, there's a good chance that Mystery is trying to get your attention. Good guides don't impose 'shoulds' or 'oughts.' Spiritual guides worth your trust can assist you in detaching from old demons and discovering inner treasures, pearls and gold hidden from awareness. We offer alternative ways of looking at change. And we carefully and caringly challenge you to view the context of your whole life with open mind and heart.

MISSING THE MYSTERY

Wall Street has become a larger-than-life economic and cultural force ever since the motto "Greed is Good!" burst into national consciousness in the 1980s. Its "masters of the universe" orchestrate mega-mergers, corporate raiders, multibillion dollar buyouts and lead opulent lives.
Walter Hamilton

In money we trust. Most of us accept money as the central focus of our life. How can it be otherwise? That's how society is planned. Advertisers exert social power because so few people have developed an awakened consciousness. Most cannot resist the pull of media. It's hard to imagine a society so awake to spiritual light and power that Wall Street and Madison Avenue become irrelevant.

How many of us are so busy keeping commitments that we lose sensitivity on the spiritual level? The din of our days dims our ability to hear the whispers of divine direction. The stuff we accumulate crowds our awareness, blotting out the touch of Love bending near. Beneath the agony and the ecstasy of owing and owning, earning and saving, giving and serving is an intrinsic and transparent Source. The Mystery of all that is

2

surrounds us and includes us, yet also eludes many of us much of the time. Spiritual guidance assists us in becoming more aware of the sacred dimension and tapping into its transforming power.

PLURIFORMITY

There is no longer a more or less Christian formation field underlying people's individual fields.　　　　　Carolyn Gratton

Few North Americans have more than a tenuous link with the faith tradition that nourished our grandparents. So many have lost touch with, and respect for, religion, no wonder we feel rootless. We're becoming a "traditionless" culture. The writer of this guide grew up Christian but today's spiritual guides and readers, like everyone else in the 21st century, are entwined in a pluriform world. Pluriformity means that the views and values of traditions as diverse as Wiccan, Native American, Jewish, Christian, Buddhist, Muslim and New Age have been in the air since most of us took our first breath. Because Providence created a veritable rainbow of races and religions, we trust that Love is at work in the creation of a whole—the pluriform field—not just the Christian part. These days the challenge of spiritual guidance lies in empowering folks to sort out what is life-giving—and what is not—from a multiplicity of faith traditions.

VULNERABILITY AND DIGNITY

Spiritual guides gently acknowledge the vulnerability of all human beings. Everyone needs and deserves respect. Everyone needs forgiveness for our own broken selves and compassion for our limitations. We all need to be treated with dignity as we attempt to wake up from the consumer-based torpor that keeps many of us sleepy, sluggish and self-centered. Spiritual awakening begins in awareness of our weakness. Most self-deception happens outside of awareness, which is why we need trustworthy friends, companions and guides to help us raise hidden inner tensions to consciousness.

"*Sin, by and large, is love gone wrong*" says Carolyn Gratton. You know what she means. Anger. Pride. Deception. Envy. Avarice. Fear. Gluttony. Lust. Sloth. Spiritual guides see all these as expressions that can be overcome through awareness, patience, willing work and grace. Human disorders involving love and money point toward an unmet longing for belonging that is missing for so many people. Yet each of us retains a personal drive to love and be loved, to know and be known. Until this inner drive is uncovered and nurtured, directed toward the good of the whole and bestowed on others, our egocentric little loves will continue to lead toward

3

disordered money lives. Spiritual guidance invites you to trust in a wisdom beyond your own and to connect with a source *"whose ways are not our ways."* (Isaiah 55:8) And finally, spiritual guidance alerts you to be alert for ways in which Love's Spirit may be addressing you.

MAKING LOVE WITH MONEY

Definitions are elusive. This guide doesn't pretend to know what "making love with money" might mean to you. Learning the mysteries of love, money and Sabbath Economics are lifelong tasks. Approaching holiness and household finance with the same gusto that we approache sexual intimacy is unusual, but not impossible. Everyone goofs up occasionally even after years of experience with lovemaking and moneymaking. The best this guide can do is to pass along some accumulated life-experience. What you do with it is up to you.

Life in Lubbock, Texas taught me two things. One is that God loves you and you're going to burn in hell. The other is that sex is the most awful, filthy thing on earth and you should save it for someone you love. Butch Hancock

Making love may have a lot to do with loving, or very little. Like sex, lovemaking means different things to different people at different times. Being an eager consumer, for example, is essential when setting up a household and not at all necessary when the nest is feathered just the way you like it. Accumulating stuff is exciting at age sixteen but boring at age sixty-six. Debt is uncomfortable when you've got a steady income but excruciating if you've lost your job. Money matters may be extremely private for people raised with family secrets yet possible to reveal when one is part of a safe group of peers who are dedicated to growth. In most long-term relationships, as in earth-advocacy groups there are stretches when activism begins to wear a person out. That's when Sabbath practices can literally be life-saving.

MATTERS OF THE HEART

Love's a fire, but whether its going to warm your heart or burn down your house, you never can tell. Joan Crawford

On an emotional level, money matters can be as powerful as you want to make them. There is no chance of making love with money without becoming emotional. The feelings that accompany financial change can be

4

fantastic. Then again, they can be totally terrible. Hopefully your money-love life will be enchanting but sometimes it won't. A hot investment can go bad and hurt so much that it leaves scars on your heart. Lovemaking with money can also be holy ground for working through all sorts of tears and fears.

READER ALERT

Most people make assumptions about the finances of other people. This guide makes no assumptions. Your belongings may fit in a backpack. Your assets may exceed the GNP of Paraguay. This guide honors your economic and spiritual life—whatever it may be- as totally unique. Whatever you own or owe, your love life and personal finances are probably too complex to be fairly represented by charts or graphs. That's why you won't find love surveys or economic projections in these pages. Most readers would probably agree that making love is most satisfying when both partners are honest, caring and fun to be around. The same is true for economic partnerships. Whatever your state or condition, this guide is rooted and grounded in full respect for your uniqueness.

This guide is not perfect, nor is it intended to be. It will not solve all your problems with love or money. There are times when it is better to put down the book and go for a walk or consult your best friend or find a meeting of Debtor's Anonymous. While the following stories, reflections and practices work well for some people, they may not interest you at all. This guide encourages you to explore aspects of personal economics that most people in this country usually aren't told about. Do with it what you will, including recycling it. I hope you find it useful enough to keep handy and consult intermittently for the next seven years. That's the average length of time it takes most of us to convert from automatic consumer habits to the daily practice of sacred economics.

CHAPTER TWO: THE GREAT INVITATION
WHERE ARE YOU?

*The supreme happiness of life is the conviction that we are loved—
loved for ourselves, or rather, loved in spite of ourselves.*
                                                        Victor Hugo

In the beginning, the Creator asked Adam and Eve *"Where are you?"* Imagine it, the first woman and man were still trying to find their way around the garden. Both were bare and barely acquainted when The Most High sought them out. Three chapters into Genesis (3:9) God initiates contact with the first couple.

Envision yourself there, relaxing under a tree, admiring Eden when you hear *"Where are you?"* What tone of voice do you hear? Is it kindly? Assuring? Intimidating? To my mind's ear the voice of God sounds warm, interested and invitational. I imagine the Source of Love still seeking relationships with people—even with me—because I trust that the Holy One genuinely wants to know what's going on with these complex creatures called humans.

The invitational perspective of this guide under-girds everything in these pages. It is rooted a hopeful, caring relationship between holy and human. *"Where are you?"* infuses all that follows.

Is A SPIRITUAL GUIDE TO SABBATH ECONOMICS: MAKING LOVE WITH MONEY your kind of book? The next twenty questions will give you a clue. Are you...

1. More attracted to questions than to answers?
2. Seeking something more that you can't quite name?
3. Financially OK now but not sure about relationships?
4. Working more and enjoying it less?
5. Spiritually alive but lukewarm about religion?
6. Experienced with love but not financially fulfilled?
7. In debt and not sure how to get out?
8. Consuming pre-packaged images and entertainment?
9. Using shopping as an anti-depressant?
10. Worrying about retirement but not saving aggressively?
11. Sending minimum payments for credit card bills?
12. Straining to stay young with diets, aerobics, cosmetics?
13. Emotionally conflicted about death and inheritance?

14. Wanting to make a living instead of making a killing?
15. Eager to apply talents and passions in right livelihood?
16. Yearning for an open 'work-style' with more free time?
17. Wondering if 'successful' means 'independently wealthy'?
18. Enjoying mutual efforts toward common goals?
19. Sensing possibilities yet to be imagined and ignited?
20. Asking "is this all there is"?

QUESTIONING: WHY READ THIS BOOK?

Where are you?   Each reader is likely to undertake the transformative work of Sabbath Economics for a different reason.   Yours could be

- o   to identify personal experiences of love and money
- o   to grow in relationship with God, self, neighbor and creation
- o   to share financial or spiritual struggles or sorrows
- o   to explore economic difficulties, dynamics or discoveries
- o   to discern the need for making changes
- o   to seek support in making difficult choices
- o   to celebrate joys or graces with love or money
- o   to test and trust inner sources of guidance
- o   to integrate spirituality into family finances

This spiritual guide encourages self-examination for individuals, households and congregations.   If you wish to pause and reflect as you read, you may want to bookmark Chapter Six—QUERIES—HEARING YOUR INNER GUIDE.   Multiple questions give ample opportunities to notice, name and describe what is true for you in the seven realms of **Slowing, Owing, Simplifying, Choosing, Giving, Belonging and Restoring**.

CHAPTER THREE
CORE CONCEPTS: SABBATH ECONOMICS

HOW MUCH IS ENOUGH?

*If one were to choose a single word to characterize the national
identity, it would have to be MORE.*   Andrew C. Bacevich

Since 1776 Americans have been passionate about life, liberty and
the pursuit of happiness. This original *"Jeffersonian trinity"* summarizes
our common inheritance and defines our common aspirations. In recent
decades, however, a new truth has become self-evident: we, the people,
have radically altered what our nation's founders meant by *"inalienable
rights"* named in The Declaration of Independence.

> *Shop til you drop.*
> *Whoever dies with the most toys wins.*
> *If it feels good, do it.*

Yes, it's true that individual Americans use freedom for countless
worthy endeavors. Many of us create and contribute, invent and invest,
rescue and restore, volunteer and vision in helping to make our country
great. But the way that we 21st century folks define *the pursuit of happiness*
has expanded along with American waistlines and national debt. More
citizens are claiming the right to consume more and acquire more while
indulging in more personal choices, more comforts and more conveniences.
Bacevich names this *"the crisis of profligacy"* and proposes that the
relentless pursuit of MORE has become the center of our national theology.

A TIME FOR RESISTANCE

*As the prerequisites of the American way of life have grown,
they have outstripped the means available to satisfy them.*
                                                Andrew C. Bacevich

Freedom in pursuit of a buck has always been central to Americans
but we've reached the point where our historical ways are no longer
sustainable. The ethic of more, the relentless pursuit of happiness through
self-gratification, now   threatens   persons,   households,   communities,
ecological systems and species across the planet. The time has come for
we, the people, to rise up and resist.

SPIRITUAL AND RELIGIOUS

Sabbath Economics is both a religious idea and a spiritual process. Traditional religion gets mixed reviews these days. Spirituality seems to hold more appeal—as in *"I'm a spiritual person but not very religious."* Religion can be a way of making sense out of a confusing world. Faith gives focus, meaning and hope to people who might otherwise have none. Spirituality can encourage belief in something beyond self. It can also be used to oppress people and to dominate nature. Maybe that's why so many folks define themselves as spiritual rather than religious. Spirituality seems roomier somehow, allowing for beliefs that oppose the greed and violence of so many forms of organized religion. The root word for religion actually means *'to tie"* or *"to link."* Sabbath Economics seeks to unite timeless religious wisdom with enduring spiritual practices in the quest to link love, money and freedom.

If you like to think that religion has no influence over personal economics, check the contents of your wallet. All currency issued by the U.S. Treasury—every coin, every bill—bears two phrases of four words each. One is "United States of America." Remember the other one?

A BASIC QUESTION: HOW MUCH IS ENOUGH?

Surplus: n. 1) An amount or quantity in excess of what is needed.   2) Total assets minus the sum of all liabilities.   3) Excess of receipts over expenditures.   Adj. Being more than or in excess of what is needed.

The American Heritage Dictionary

Great power for change emerges when Sabbath practices—**meditation, prayer and reflection**—are united with money matters—**debt, saving, giving and investing**—and tied to lifestyle issues—**eating, accumulating, simplifying, neighboring and greening.** Great change is already happening in households where some form of Sabbath Economics is practiced. Such freeing ways of change are also possible for you and for those you love.

Perhaps you were drawn to the title because you seek ease, balance and joy in money matters. Perhaps you are ready to become more of a change agent. Uniting elemental powers of **earth, air, fire and water** with financial choices can be a truly transformative combination, and transformative people are surely needed at this time in history. Reclaiming the meaning of biblical elements—**breath, seed, salt, light, pearl, gold**—and linking their powers with personal economics can enrich material situations, enliven spiritual conditions, elevate the common good and energize planetary healing.

The following chapters include stories from the author's Sabbath Economics journey along with those of women, men and faith-based communities choosing to unite love with money in many different ways. Core concepts are drawn from sacred scripture, poetry and theology. Spiritual practices invite individuals, couples and groups to delve deeper. Queries extend the spirit of invitation—*"Where are you?"* with provocations nudging readers to dive deep in exploring habits and values from personal, familial, biblical, communal and global perspectives

LET US SEE WHAT LOVE CAN DO

Love is the central teaching and core truth of most world religions.
You shall love the Lord your God with all your heart, with all your soul and with all your mind.   *Matthew 22:37*

The great invitation of Jesus beckons us to see how we can link love with money. This guide celebrates the ancient invitation of loving toward the purpose of expanding personal awareness and drawing more of us toward greater consciousness. Sabbath Economics is a lifelong process which begins by reflecting deeply on our own financial and spiritual realities and resisting what is no longer life-giving. Gradually, as we bring more economic truths to mind and gather more spiritual truths to heart, we begin to recognize grace at work in more subtle and surprising ways. We may discover how Spirit has been guiding our choices behind the scenes, how love has been awaiting our attention, how a richer relationship with Holy Presence is already under way. Greater financial and relational freedom is possible through inner work, whether you participate in a religious congregation or not. Love, money and freedom seek you wherever you are.

A WORD FROM OUR FOUNDER

Ched Myers has worked as a "theological animator" for more than three decades. He is committed to nonviolent activism for social justice, church renewal and radical discipleship working across the theological spectrum with groups large and small, grassroots and institutional, activist and ecclesial. In 1997 Ched and several colleagues established Bartimeus Collaborative Ministries as a platform for their educational and organizing efforts.

In 2001 The Church of the Savior in Washington, DC published Ched Myer's *THE BIBLICAL VISION OF SABBATH ECONOMICS*, a popular booklet that continues to be widely used as a study tool. This guide stays close to the root of Ched's witness and work, extending his teachings with more emphasis on Sabbath and self-discovery, adapting his original covenant for readers who want to link personal economics with sacred practices. Here Ched focuses on self-chosen limits as he describes the essence of a Sabbath Economics Household Covenant:

"We the people must limit our economic activity in order to keep the gifts of creation circulating equitably. Today's challenge: *The terrible but inevitable consequences of our current way of life are the twin global apocalypses of the broadening environmental crisis and the deepening gulf between rich and poor.* Earth citizens today face staggering statistics about escalating wars and tribal tyranny, environmental degradation, rampant abuses of human rights and generational violence rooted in poverty. The problems are overwhelming.

> Where do we begin restoring the goodness of creation?
> What might you and I do now?

Ched Myers points toward five essential lifestyle dimensions:

1- THE LAND.
   Which natural places do you care about enough to defend?
   Start there, with a backyard garden, regional park, local streambed or beloved national park.

2- THE POOR.
   The truth of any society is not found in the rich and beautiful but in those who suffer hunger and sickness. Their faces show grace in the struggle to survive. Privileged folks need to learn who the indigenous people of our area were and are, and to face the ways they suffer from dispossession that benefits us.

3- OUR MONEY.
   Examine how my household and congregation handles surplus. Consider investing it in communities that are most in need of capital.

4- OUR POSSESSIONS.
   Until we realize that stuff cannot make us happy, we won't be able to recover from the consumer attachments that drive the destructive ideology of growth.

11

5- OUR WORK.
   How do I earn my bread?   Being anxious about money and fretting
   about work kidnap our attention and energy.   Vitality rises when we
   find vocation through discipleship.   Identity need not be limited to
   what we do for a living or what we own.

   The respected founder of the Sabbath Economics movement adapted
by countless households and adopted by varied communities, sums it up:

> *My hope is that we will acknowledge our profound need for Sabbath*
> *to do this kind of examination.   Sabbath time and space help us*
> *muster the character and courage to make changes.   Our struggle*
> *against a sick system, however, can only be animated and sustained*
> *by commitment to a community of life.   In the long run, people make*
> *hard personal choices and take on difficult political tasks only in the*
> *context of the love, accountability and celebration of the church—*
> *that is, a congregation transformed by the biblical vision of Sabbath*
> *Economics.*   *Ched Myers*

CHAPTER FOUR
SABBATH REST: DEPTHS and HEIGHTS

FROM LEARNED LABOR TO ORIGINAL REST

Set thine own house in order.
2 Kings 20:1, KJV

TGIF! How many of us have heard or said *Thank God it's Friday !* as we left the work place? *TGIF!* is a widely-shared expression of relief in our culture. Thank God the work week is winding down! But we wonder, does the pace of public and private life ever really slow down? How many of us are accustomed to enjoying life at a Sabbath's pace?

Those who honor the Sabbath are in the minority. It has become rather quaint to set aside a day of rest to rejoice in the Holy Presence. Most 21st-century folks seem to work most of the time. *Time is money*, or so we say, a handy cliché to justify the restless pace we keep. Working hard to consume pre-packaged leisure activities, many of us miss the spirit of Sabbath. Body and soul get depleted, along with heart and mind. Forgetting the lightness of being, we remember the weight of obligations. Neglecting to take our imaginations out to play, we become bereft of creative ideas. Taking time to savor a memory from a friend's funeral seems as outdated as a porch swing. Deprived of Sabbath, we get no rest. Busy-ness rules our days. Time becomes a bullet train that rushes us from one place to another.

FROM EFFORTFUL STRIVING to SABBATH LOVING

The older I get the slower my body moves, echoing the wind-up clock beside my childhood bed. Rhythmic tick-tocks comforted me then, subliminally echoing my mother's heartbeat. As I slipped into sleep, the peaceful quality of prenatal life enfolded me. I wonder if the desire for Sabbath rest began in the womb while our tiny human forms were being infused with pure Essence. I wonder if unconscious memories of God's Being might have inspired the ancient Hebrews (*Deuteronomy 5:12-13*) to declare:

"Observe the Sabbath day by keeping it holy, as the Lord your God, has commanded you. Six days you shall labor and do all your work, but the seventh day is a Sabbath to the Lord Your God. On it you shall do no work... or to have inspired the Psalmist to praise God (*Psalm 139:13-14*):

For it was you who formed my inward parts;
You knit me together in my mother's womb.
I praise you, for I am fearfully and wonderfully made.

C.G. Jung tells of a native African who was invited by American visitors to get into a car and take a drive with them. After half an hour the passenger asked the driver to stop. He stepped out and stretched himself on the ground beside the road. They asked if he was sick. No, he felt alright, but he had to wait for his soul to catch up. The car had gone too fast and his soul got left behind. The pace of our secular society does seem to race ahead of soul time. Sabbath practices and Sabbath economics keep soul and body together, and help us notice when distance grows between the two.

FROM EMPTY SEPARATION
to SACRED CONNECTION

The dual purpose of life is to cultivate wealth and to strengthen personal ego, right? American culture and economy both seem to say so. Secular social forces reinforce individual autonomy, subtly working to enhance and maintain personal ego, conspiring to convince me that I must work hard to accumulate more material security and success. Such an individualized way of life puts enormous pressure on you and me even during so-called leisure time. Most people feel doubly driven. Society compels us to inwardly build up our sense of self-worth while economics compels us to outwardly build up our financial assets. When this dual pressure gets to be too much, we tend to collapse into oblivion through food, TV, sleep, sex, alcohol, drugs or whatever gets us numb for awhile. How many of us bounce between some form of driven achievement, on and off the job, and some form of mind-numbing private escape? Given this crazed socio-economic rhythm, is it any wonder that we wind up feeling anxious and empty?

Emptiness comes in two forms, sacred and scary. Inner emptiness allows us to explore the truth of ourselves, whatever that might be. Sacred emptiness readies us to receive more goodness and mercy than we can imagine, but first we may need to pass through the valley of the shadow of death. Scary emptiness brings up a sense of unease or maybe of dread. Unstructured time may leave us feeling bad, deficient, not-okay with ourselves. Poking around my inner emptiness during Sabbath quiet, I may notice that my insides aren't empty at all. I may discover that my gut is full of uncomfortable stuff—old hurts, memories of shame, feelings of neglect, painful childhood moments and adult regrets. Scary emptiness may pipe up in a small, shameful, scolding voice:

14

"Uh-oh.   I haven't accomplished enough,
I haven't accumulated enough,
And I am not enough."

BEING, DOING, HAVING ENOUGH
ESTHER ELIZABETH SPEAKS HER TRUTH

"How much is enough?"   *I have wrestled with this question for decades and it permeates everything—what I do, how I live, how I interpret the gospel, what actions and policies I support, how I treat the earth and others.* How much is enough? *filters through every aspect of my life. How I answer it affects my spiritual well-being and the well-being of the world.*

DEMONS

It is not enough said her dad to
Win the sports tournament
Take first place in the speech contest
You must become
The boy I wanted

It is not enough said her mother to
Graduate with honors
You must visit your dying grandmother
And fulfill the dreams I had for myself

It is not enough said her husband to
Give up your identity
You must be the managing director
Of my domain

It is not enough said her child
That you make cookies for school functions
And be a soccer mom
You must give up your life
And tend to mine

It is not enough said her minister
That you give your life to Jesus
You must teach Sunday School classes
Serve on all the committees
And organize the food bank

It is not enough "they" said
It is not enough
You are not enough
We need more of you

She became very very tired
As the demons in her head
Continued to claim her life
And dry rot her soul

One day
While sitting under a tree
These words were whispered
In her being

It is all a lie

She stood up
And began twirling around and around
While demons left
And angels sang
She kept on dancing
And
As her soul was restored
She claimed her life.

BEING ENOUGH—HAVING ENOUGH

Everyone I know wants to be enough. Hardly anyone I know believes they are enough. I wonder at times, many times really, if I am intelligent, gifted, sufficient, or worthy enough. Am I courageous, clever, funny, strong, or loving enough? The list goes on and on and on and on... I am not alone in this wondering. Somewhere, somehow, most of us have embraced the notion that we are insufficient, flawed, and inadequate. I believe nearly everything we say and do is affected, informed, and influenced by this notion.

While I believe the human spirit hungers to be enough, I also believe that I (and most likely you) deal with the fear of not being enough by cluttering and busying my life, running as fast as I can doing, doing, doing so I will not be found out, so I will appear to be valuable, so no one will notice all the ways I am deficient. This compulsive doing, achieving, owning, and having zaps my energy, dries up my creative juices, leaves me emotionally drained, spiritually unfulfilled, physically exhausted, and joyless. None of my doing or having can or will fill the hole in my soul caused by the conviction that I am not enough.

As a child of the Christian tradition, I wrestle with the demons that have been implanted in my head about how God wants more of me, expect me to do more: feed more hungry people, work harder for justice, visit more people in prison, and take care of more neighbors. The list of all I should do is endless. The Christian message I embodied (which is not the message I now believe) is clear—"In God's eye I will always have to be something more than I am and to do something more than I am doing."

As a child of North American culture, it is hard for me to truly be at peace with who I am or what I have. I live in a society that is ever-restless, always eager for more mountains to climb, always seeking happiness through accomplishing and accumulating. I do not have to go too far or think too hard to discover where this notion of not being enough comes from. I am fed this message every single day of my life. In just one day I counted forty-nine advertisements that suggested that, as a woman, I "lack" something I could acquire easily by going on this diet, wearing that line of clothing, driving this model of car, or scheduling an appointment to have my face and bosom lifted and my wrinkles flattened out.

In truth, it matters little where I received this notion of not being enough. What matters is whether I believe it. This notion is a lie. And the lie holds us in bondage. I have noticed something profoundly disturbing. When I feel flawed, deficient, not good enough, I tend to look at others through this same lens. When I am around others who reveal that they feel insufficient and inadequate, I wonder if they want more of me than I'm able or willing to offer them.

I have also noticed that I use my feelings of festering inadequacy to justify my actions. I can excuse myself for not doing certain things, for saying "no" to invitations I am called to say "yes" to, or for not taking certain risks. OR I can prove I really am enough by saying "yes" to nearly everything, things I should say "no" to, things that do not make my heart sing, that end up dry-rotting my soul. I know how to hide behind "not good enough" and play it safe, be the victim, estrange myself from people I want to be close to, and remain helpless and passive. But what and whom does this really serve?

I want to be resurrected, brought back from the dead. I want to live life fully, believing in my gut that I am the beloved; that I am made in the image of God; that even as I continue to grow into wholeness, I am—right now, in each and every moment—enough.

I have, on rare occasions, felt enough. These times usually take place when I am grounded in my relationship with God; when I have turned my will over to the care of God as I understand God; when I have gotten out of the way and allowed the Spirit to move through me. In this place of enough-ness, I experience a deep sense of well-being; I know in my gut that very little is needed to make a happy life; I understand that nothing really matters outside of honest, loving relationships with God, others, and myself; and I reside in the truth that "all will be well, and all will be well, all manner of thing shall be well." (Julian of Norwich)

My deepest hunger is to reside in this realm of being enough the majority of time, if not all the time. And I don't. Even so, the wind is blowing and the Spirit is moving, informing me of some deep truths. When I embrace these truths, I believe I will be transformed, resurrected, called out of my tomb, and moved beyond my sense of not being enough.

SPIRIT TRUTHS

I have been taught that I am somehow defective. This is a lie.

Perfectionism is a myth, never a reality. I am to be faithful, not perfect.

I am empowered when I empower others.

When I own my goodness and belovedness, I can more easily see these qualities in others.

It is a good thing to do less in order to carve out more space to be.

I do not deserve the "grace" I am offered, and I will receive it graciously.

The God I believe in is a liberating God. I do not have to do anything else or have anything else to be accepted for who I am.

If the derelicts and ragamuffins Jesus hung out with had enough and were good enough for Jesus, then so am I.

Let it be so—amen and amen.

Esther Elizabeth, 2007

THE GREAT INVITATION:
THROUGH EMPTINESS to ESSENCE

Spiritual emptiness has its difficult moments but gifts of enough-ness make the effort worth the challenge. Jesus and Buddha sought it. Alone in wilderness, forest, garden, mountaintop or boat, they practiced a form of self-emptying known as *kenosis*. Sabbath emptiness invites us into direct experience of freedom, touching Essence where everything is enough and I, too, am enough. When we humans stop working so much and get quiet inside, surprising blessings flow from the Source of Life. When we allow universal Light to clear our minds of brilliant ideas, mental clarity can illuminate our concerns. When we invite Love to empty our hearts of emotionally-charged inner dialogues, Transforming Power can ease difficult relationships. When we allow Sabbath rest to support us in detaching our attention from bodily sensations, Holy Spirit can restore physical aliveness. When we give our will a rest from planning tomorrow's agenda, divine guidance points us toward next steps on the path of right action.

Essence refers to the inner seed, to divine elements at the core of each human being. Jesus introduced four dimensions of essence in a teaching that bible editors called The Great Commandment (Luke 10:25-28). This guide prefers to think of this teaching as The Great Invitation since the ministry of Jesus was essentially invitational. You and I are invited into the fourfold wholeness of loving self and neighbor – near and far neighbors, known and unknown neighbors – as we love God – with all our heart, soul, mind and will. Eugene Peterson's Message, a contemporary version of the Bible, translates is this way: "Love the Lord your God with all your passion and prayer and muscle and intelligence – and love your neighbor as well as you do yourself."

Scripture writers testify to something that infuses people with joy, compassion and patience. Prophets tell of ordinary women and men who shine with honesty, generosity and peace. Psalms praise God for gifts of intellect, imagination and vision, expressing wonder for the pleasures of sight, hearing, taste and touch. Passion, prayer, muscle and intelligence can work together in mature persons. Inward listening invites love in, freeing the will to receive intuitive guidance and take right action.

FROM SECULAR DOING to SABBATH BEING

The Sabbath is a bride, and its celebration is like a wedding.
Abraham Joshua Heschel

The word 'Sabbath' comes from the Hebrew verb *shabat*, which means *'to rest or stop working.'* Delighting after six incredible days of creating (*Genesis 2:2*) God rests. The Creator of the cosmos established a primal pattern of good work followed by rest.

> *"This cosmic Sabbath was not for the purpose of resting in order to work more; there is no Monday in the Creation narrative. The purpose of this Sabbath is to enjoy the world forever, which is why it is blessed."* Ched Myers

Honoring the Sabbath gives people more than the righteous satisfaction of obeying an ancient commandment. The inner stillness of Sabbath opens seeds of Essence so that loving-kindness can circulate through our bloodstreams. Sabbath rest cracks shells of fear so that seeds of trust can grow. Restful reflection eases ego's grip, healing old deficiencies and erasing old masks. Keeping the Sabbath holy invites the shy soul to emerge from the seed, to share its spiritual gifts, to become as fresh and vivid as a child. Playing and praying loosens the grip of social conventions, eases the hold of economic forces and releases goodness and mercy in the world.

True Sabbath may not be easy to attain at first. Sabbath practitioners need commitment to stay with it, since inner states of deficient emptiness and spacious emptiness are constantly changing places on the dance floor of consciousness. Those who remain faithful to Sabbath practices affirm that regular rest and reflection does faithfully nourish the body, restore the soul, illuminate the mind, untangle the emotions, free the ego from social pressure and release personal finances from patterns of over-spending and under-giving.

A CONTEMPLATIVE SABBATH PRACTICE:
FREE TO ACCOMPLISH NOTHING

How beautiful it is to do nothing and then rest afterward.
Spanish proverb

If my Puritan ancestors had heard this proverb they would have dismissed it. My forefathers and mothers were Scot/English farmers, truckers, cooks and gardeners who extolled the virtues of hard work and self-denial. Along with fair skin I inherited the motto *"Be useful, not just decorative."* Children in my blue-collar, working-class family were instructed to *"Keep busy or at least look busy."* Doing nothing is quite a challenge for me. How about you?

In memory of my steady, sturdy ancestors, I choose to accomplish nothing today. Your mission, should you choose to accept it, is to accomplish nothing either. Just for today, join me in practicing The Great Invitation. Can you enjoy a do-nothing day or at least a do-nothing evening?

How? If nothing-doing seems totally impossible, play with some simple variations. Let eye muscles relax as you watch grass grow. Let ear canals rest as you listen to melodic music. Let hands stretch as you play with a yo-yo. Let brain strain dissolve as you gaze at the sky. Find a place where you can stand comfortably on the earth, a spot where you won't be disturbed for awhile. Take off your shoes and go barefoot if you like. Plant your feet a comfortable width apart, let your body find its center of gravity and simply enjoy being rooted and grounded on earth. Notice what comes up for you. Take as much time as you like or need. Invite imagination to be your guide or curl up and take a nap.

Henry David Thoreau became quite accomplished at accomplishing nothing. When peers accused him of idleness, he described its deep virtues in *Walden.* Playfully reversing the ancient wisdom recorded in The Book of Genesis, Thoreau declared: *"It was morning, and lo, now it is evening and nothing memorable is accomplished."* Thoreau's enduring words testify to the myriad, mysterious ways in which *nothing* is transformed into *something* during open, unstructured times. Letting go of busy agendas is very freeing. Accomplishing nothing lets us discover our true place— personally, relationally, economically, environmentally and spiritually—as we honor Sabbath time and keep it holy.

SABBATH REFLECTION:
FROM SECULAR EFFORT TO SABBATH EASE

Love the Lord your God with all your heart, with all your
soul, with all your strength, and with all your mind,   and
your neighbor as yourself.   Luke 10:27, JB

Personal peace and global justice are rooted in economically stable households. Given the relative affluence and freedom of many North Americans, new options are becoming possible. At this time in history, you and I have multiple claims on our time. We know of many ways to use the resources entrusted to us. Multi-ethnic and multi-religious perspectives abound, revealing varied ways of loving God, self, neighbor and planet.

Sabbath renewal is both the center and the circumference of the Sabbath Economics Household Covenant. We are invited to pay equal attention to the money issues of **debt, saving, giving, investing** and to the lifestyle issues of **consumption, living green** and **neighboring in solidarity with people on the margins of society.** We will focus on each in the following chapters.

DESIGNING YOUR OWN
SABBATH ECONOMICS COVENANT

Love…with all your passion and prayer and intelligence…
And love others as well as you love yourself.
                          Matthew 23:37-39, (*The Message*)

A covenant is a binding agreement made between people and the Holy. A Sabbath Economics Household Covenant invites us to link love with money and to couple intention with attention. It means enfolding financial choices and lifestyle issues in the mantle of Sabbath rest. A covenant is a useful guide and a tool of spiritual maturity. The details of your Sabbath Economics Household Covenant will look different than mine because our households are different and our ideas are, too. Today's covenant may be different tomorrow because fiscal realities change once we undertake Sabbath Economics practices.

Designing a covenant encourages us to choose more responsive ways to use our treasure and our time. It beckons us toward more satisfying ways to contribute our talent and our tenderness. Countless households and communities have become committed to Sabbath Economics and find it a worthy discipline. Developing a Household Covenant puts each of us in the company of good people who choose a balanced life of work, rest, play and service in order to create a better world for all.

Folks committed to Sabbath-based household economics confirm that the monetary elements of the Covenant—**eliminating debt, community investing** and **generous giving**—can be very challenging in our time. Adding the focus on lifestyle elements of **conscious consumption, green living** and **neighboring with marginalized people** makes Sabbath Economics even more complex. Simplicity and solidarity are difficult to achieve and maintain in our consumer culture. Most folks cannot stay with such a challenging program without solid community support. Putting Sabbath first, setting rest and spiritual renewal at the center of each week, gives spiritual circumference to our choices. The Sabbath Economics Household Covenant then becomes not only possible, but delightfully freeing. Time with the sacred nourishes the human soul better than anything for sale at the mall or on E-Bay.

A Sabbath Economics covenant requires a high commitment, beyond what your peers may be willing to venture. You and I will work out very different forms of relationship with love, money, faith and practice. Fiscal freedom looks different to each of us, defined by our own gifts and limits, within our own communities.

Then you will know the truth, and the truth will set you free…
so if Love sets you free, you will be free indeed.

John 8:32,26 NIV

THE FIRST DIMENSION
SABBATH: SLOWING   HEED YOUR SEED

> *Apples grow from apple seeds.*
> *Humans grow from God seeds.*
>
> Meister Eckhart

A divine seed of being dwells deep within, a seed is as unique as your fingerprint. Trauma and suffering can wither it or nourish its growth. Resting and remembering can release hidden hurts. Sabbath practices pair personal possibilities with transpersonal powers that come to our assistance.

Financial guidance sprouts within the rhythm of creation when subliminal rhythms of Sabbath strengthen us to make life-enhancing choices with time, energy, imagination, service, creativity, love and money. Richard Lowery sums it up: *Sabbath thus captures the double theme of the creation story: abundance as the divine gift and self-limitation as the appropriate response.*

THE SECOND DIMENSION
DEFICIT: OWING   BE YOUR LIGHT

> *What is to give light must endure burning.*
> Viktor Frankl

Simply put, debt enslaves people. Financial and emotional deficit keeps debtors in bondage. You and I are granted freedom in the choices we make about owing, owning, spending, keeping, serving, giving, investing, neighboring and restoring a healthy planet. The power to get out of debt emerges from a spiritual source, not a social one.

THE THIRD DIMENSION
STUFF: SIMPLIFYING   KINDLE YOUR FIRE

> *All of you are kindlers of fire, lighters of firebrands.*
> *Walk in the flame of your fire and among the*
> *brands that you have kindled.*   Isaiah 50:11

The core meaning of *"spirituality"* is defined as *energy or life force.* Understandings of self, stuff and Sabbath tend to be warm or cool under different conditions. A Spiritual Guide to Sabbath Economics invites you to come in from the cold but not to stand back from the heat. The seven-fold household covenant leads from second-hand learning to direct knowing and from there may lead you into the fiery furnace of fiscal and social change. Transforming fire kindles the desire to risk more.

THE FOURTH DIMENSION
FOOD: CHOOSING   BE THE BREAD

> *How could you fail to perceive that I was not speaking about bread?*   Gospel of Matthew 16:11

Mixing Sabbath practices into money matters and lifestyle choices lifts the loaf of our common life. Prayer is the yeast that suffuses saving, giving and investing with goodness. Meditative practices infuse lifestyle choices of consuming, sharing and restoring with generosity toward self and neighbor

THE FIFTH DIMENSION
SURPLUS: GIVING   KNOW YOUR FLOW

> *2.5 million dollars is the amount of surplus that average Americans say they would need to "feel rich."*
> Money Magazine, May 2005

Communication with the Ultimate frees folks from holding onto wealth, connects us with The Holy More and releases us to give more. Some folks pray verbally—*Hello, sun. Good morning, tree.* Some pray quietly with breath alone. Larry Dossey sums it up: *"Prayer is what it needs to be."* What is your form?

THE SIXTH DIMENSION
NEIGHBORING: BELONGING   SAVOR YOUR SALT

> *He said "Bring me a new bowl and put salt in it."* 2 Kings 2:20

Sacred practices can be like new bowls of awareness. Ancient forms of meditation and prayer offer time and space to gather spiritual gifts that outlast old hurts. Salt seasons and preserves foods; it invites us to pause and savor the taste of Presence. When we slow down we become free to receive the More. And it is good. It is very good. Like many analogies, the phrase *"Savor your salt"* may be intriguing or confusing. What might salt have to do with neighboring? Belonging? What will you discover?

THE SEVENTH DIMENSION
EARTHCARE: RESTORING   BREATHE YOUR AIR

As simple as it sounds, attentive breathing is the microscopic shift behind stupendous events. Self-centered thoughts stop whirling when we focus on breathing. Self-preoccupied feelings stop whining. Background quiet finds expression. Prayer is born. What is prayer, if not the sole stable point—a point of peace and light—in this complex universe? Breathing in the present moment, and knowing that we are breathing, is the radiant "place" where Love is present.

CHAPTER FIVE
MONEY-LOVE STORIES: A GRANDMOTHER'S PEARLS

*The kingdom of heaven is like a merchant in search of a
fine pearl; On finding one pearl of great value he went and
sold all that he had and bought it.*   Matthew 13:45-46

The author begins her reflections with a personal parable in the
manner of the man from Nazareth: Consider the pearl, a treasure to behold.
Consider the source, a humble bivalve mollusk that dwells on the ocean
floor and does its work in darkness. Oysters don't set out to produce pearls
because they want the satisfaction of creating something beautiful. Oysters
are trying to get comfortable and stay comfortable. Pearls don't set out to be
valuable. They start out as simple grains of sand. But when these two get
together, when bits of sand get inside shells, then oysters get irritated.
Oysters react to discomfort by secreting something to coat the annoying
grain of sand until it becomes less bothersome. Oysterly persistence is what
brings pearls into being. Economic freedom also requires loving labor.

DESIRE TO ACQUIRE

*To find the pearl one must calm the waves;
    It's hard to find if one stirs up the water.*
                                 Mumom Rahada Roshi

The open secret of transformation is that personal change works like
oyster-pearl formation. The desire to acquire begins very early in North
American children. Economic irritants build up as youth grow up. These
irritants almost always include financial confusion and unconscious habits
that keep us captive to the seductions of consumer culture. The unchecked
desire to acquire can tyrannize people like us without our even noticing it.
Automatic spending, accumulating stuff and piling up debt can go on until a
person becomes aware that something is off kilter.
   Denial is my favorite coping response. *What problem? Not mine.*
This hardy defense pattern worked for a long time, keeping me in the dark
about what was driving my behavior and therefore blithely unaware of the
mounting financial, relational and spiritual costs.   Happy in my shell,
soothing the irritants with small comforts, I could merrily eat, drink and re-
marry. And I did.
   What, me change?

Transformation is triggered when the level of unease that results from consumerist activities exceeds the degree of ease. Unfulfilled desires turn into irritants after awhile, the kind of itch that no amount of fiscal scratching can soothe. The endless cycle of wanting, shopping, getting, losing and debt eventually threatens personal comfort. Like the gradual transformation from sand to pearl, human economic change is a byproduct of irritation and struggle.

WHERE AM I? WRITING WHAT IS TRUE

"Writing is for me a way of understanding what is happening to me, of thinking hard things out. I've never written a book that was not born out of a question I needed to answer for myself."   May Sarton

May Sarton is my kind of writer. We're a lot alike except that she is famous and I'm not, but I resonate with her views and values. Even though I did write (and rewrite) this Spiritual Guide to Sabbath Economics, I am NOT an expert on household economics. Quite the opposite: I struggle with numerical dyslexia. This means that confusion floods my mind when I hear or see numbers. Math was tough in elementary school, confounding in high school and so terrifying in graduate school that I made it through statistics only with the help of a paid tutor.

So no, I did not write this guide because I understand economics. I write to sort out some of my confusions and hopefully, to address some of yours. I also write as a way to harvest the fruits of my lifelong struggle with money. I liken the act of writing to mining for gold in that it unearths unhealthy money messages buried deep beneath consciousness. Or, to mix metaphors, writing is also like diving deep and surfacing. Both are hard work and can be dangerous as real gold miners and pearl divers will testify. Metaphorical deep-diving is safer than the physical kind but it also takes guts, grace, grit and great dedication.

Like other prayerful writers I deal with emotional, physical, mental, financial and spiritual discomfort by writing about what is bothering me. Economic irritants include unconscious habits that kept me captive to consumer culture, to personal and national debt and to the tyranny of global corporations. These are modern versions of what scripture calls "the principalities and powers."

When I can't figure out how to get free from overpowering forces, I can always turn life's irritants into stories. The personal reflections that follow are not gems on the scale of pure gold or perfect pearl, but I value them enough to offer a few to you. You—the reader—get to decide if there are gems of wisdom here and to discern what value—if any—my pearls have in your own work with love and money

SEED: THE FIRST ELEMENT
    PARENTS: GOOD SEEDS, SOME WEEDS

> *"The soul's greatest desire is to see goodness."*
> Bernard of Clairvaux

I was born in Oregon to a family of modest means. They earned daily bread as farmers, truckers, loggers, electricians, cooks and secretaries. They fed us blue-collar values along with Cream of Wheat and macaroni and cheese. When bombs fell on Pearl Harbor I was teething and just beginning to toddle when my young uncles donned Air Force uniforms and went overseas. The sirens and sacrifices of World War Two shaped my early childhood.

A broken eardrum kept my father out of the Army. His contribution to the war effort meant rising at three AM, catching a bus to work, loading his milk truck with dairy products and delivering fresh milk to the porches of Portland. Before the Teamsters unionized milkmen there were no health benefits and no vacations. Dad earned barely enough money to keep a roof over our heads. Mom cooked over a wood stove, literally keeping the home fires burning to warm, feed, clothe and guide three children born in less than five years. She managed the household with remarkable patience and goodwill.

My parents, deeply scarred by The Great Depression, sacrificed to provide my brothers and me with greater freedom in work and play, love and money than they themselves enjoyed. Much of their money story was unknown to me until late in life. As he approached death my Dad confessed that soon after he married Mom he overspent by building a house beyond his means. Wanting a snug nest for his family, desiring the very best that the building trade had to offer in 1940, Dad kept adding features during construction. By the time the house was finished it cost more than he could pay. Telling this story sixty years after the loss, his face still flushed with the humiliation of bankruptcy, losing his lovely house to bank repossession. But my father only made that mistake once. From then on my parents struggled to get out of debt and labored to stay out of debt. Planning, scrimping, saving and investing became a way of life. Their dedication led to putting kids through college and loaning start-up funds for homes and businesses.

I was taught to earn, own, spend, save and give responsibly. Thanks to my parents' choices I enjoyed enough economic and emotional surplus to develop empathy for people who are burdened by poverty. Thanks to my church-going grandmother I received enough early spiritual guidance to develop compassion for folks who are blessed—and burdened—with wealth. Now I pass this legacy of love and money along to readers and your heirs.

SPROUTING THE SEED

Other seeds fell on good soil and brought forth grain.
Matthew 13:8

About the time I learned to sing *Jesus loves me, this I know"* Grandma assured me: *"Jesus is your friend. Remember that you are a baptized child and that Christ will always look after you."*

Did I remember? Yes, for awhile. During Dad's alcoholic rages I climbed into the safety of my top bunk, covered my head with a blanket and asked Jesus to protect Mom, my little brothers and me. And he did. When the crisis passed my prayer would become less fervent and more automatic, simply repeating the lines of *"Now I lay me down to sleep."* Jesus faded into the background as I grew and got busy with school, camp and college. Chapel attendance was required in the 1950s at Congregational-based Pacific University. I went along with the program for awhile, then questioned religious authority and eventually concluded that nothing life-giving was to be found in the traditional church.

About the time The Beatles recorded *Abbey Road* I took a new road to Shasta Abbey. Burdened with wifely and motherly responsibilities my shy soul-seed was hidden so deep that I barely knew I had one. I sensed that there must be more to life than this but had no idea what it was or how to find it. Learning to meditate seemed like a good start. Following the counsel of a Zen friend I took a weekend retreat at a monastic community on Mt. Shasta. Tired of dominant males telling me what to do, I turned to a woman abbot to introduce me to the art and practice of Buddhist meditation.

Am amazing moment happened one Saturday morning as I sat in silence with the monks. I was too scattered to focus on more than three breaths in a row. The goal was to count to ten but I never did make it. While trying to clear my busy mind and untangle my troubled emotions light suddenly flooded me, a powerful loving Light too awesome to comprehend. Trembling before such great Presence I remember feeling grateful that I was already sitting on the floor for surely I would have fallen as Moses did before the burning bush.

Suffused with light and completely confused, I heard a firm, warm voice:

These are not your saints.
Come unto me.

29

What?

What is The Light of the World doing addressing me in a zendo?
　　Is this merciful voice inviting me to come unto Christ?
　　　　If not Jesus then who …a bodhisatva perhaps?

　　Vibrant with Love but not understanding what was going on, I sat stunned on my zafu, embraced by greater joy and peace than I had ever imagined possible. Entranced by Light, my thoughts bounced, totally confused …What just happened? I tried to reason it out. *"These are not your saints"* must mean that I was not to follow the Buddhist lineage of Roshi Jiyu Kennett. The next words—*"come unto me"*—carried great intensity. I kept puzzling over what it could mean.

　　At the monastery I didn't dare ask the roshi about all this. At home there was no one to confide in. My experience had been so odd and yet so compelling that I feared being labeled crazy. I might have sought pastoral counseling if I'd had a pastor. At that age, late twenties, I was far too restless to sit in church, too bored by sermons and too modern to open the Bible. I had no idea then how central Sabbath is to Christians and Jews, and yet had stumbled into some sort of Sabbath by going to the zendo.

　　Something was eating at me, making me restless. I sensed an inchoate drive toward something more, something beyond my horizon. I felt incomplete but had no idea what was missing. It was the search for this elusive something, this mysterious pearl of great price, that had led me to a Zen monastery in the first place. In the company of Buddhists I was addressed by what seemed like the Living Christ. What am I to do with all this? Better just forget it…But I couldn't forget it. *Love that would not let me go* led me to join a church, seek counsel with a woman pastor, and leave the comforts of home to study at seminary,

NURTURING THE SEED

You are to love the Lord your God with all your heart,
with all your soul, with all your energy, and with all your
mind; and your neighbor as yourself.　　Luke 10:27 SV

　　Soon after completing my M.Div. degree at Pacific School of Religion, I enrolled in a spiritual direction program at Shalem Institute for Spiritual Formation in Washington, DC. Tilden Edwards, Rosemary Dougherty and Gerald May became trusted spiritual guides. Jerry listened attentively to what had happened two decades earlier at Shasta Abbey. He thought mine had been a *"unitive experience."* God, he assured me, is an equal-opportunity inviter. May's research revealed that the Holy One seems

30

to approach everyone directly in different ways, ages and places, touching the smart and the slow, the rich and the poor, the young and the old. Some are too overwhelmed to consciously recall the encounter. Some cannot hold such magnificent magnitude and dismiss the experience as weird. Some souls are open and eager to accept the Divine Presence but have no one to confide it to, so the gift remains hidden in the heart. Folks like me wrestle with the meanings of a Great Invitation in the privacy of our journals until a spiritual guide provides a safe place to revisit, absorb and respond to the wonder of it all. One unitive experience at Shasta Abbey still lights the way, prompting me to learn Tibetan Buddhist forms of mindfulness meditation, to practice Christian forms of contemplative prayer and to enjoy Sufi dance and Native American forms of earthy reverence.

The hidden seed of my true self cracked open when The Great Invitation became close and personal. The voice I heard in the zendo infused me with Light so powerful and Love so fiery that it set my life on a new course. The Holy Spirit led me into (and later out of) pastoral ministry, in a lifelong vocation of holy companionship and prayer-based work for economic justice.

LIGHT: THE SECOND ELEMENT
MY STORY of LIFE, DEBT and DIVORCE

The borrower is slave to the lender.   Proverbs 22:7

Thinking back, it seems that life and debt must have bonded in my amniotic fluid. Born radiant like most babies, my infancy was soon shadowed by foreclosure. My parents' marriage had been founded on debt and their union nearly foundered when the house they built to welcome me was repossessed by the bank. Mother's milk contained so much sorrow and shame that it seems as if my baby bones absorbed maternal unworthiness along with calcium.

At age nineteen I left my parents home to marry a good man who had very different views and values. He mortgaged and leveraged our modest assets in a fierce pursuit of wealth. After twenty years I left the marriage when community-property debts exceeded my capacity to bear the weight. Love and money almost came to blows, but we divorced instead of getting into a fist-fight.

Primal fear of debt reached a crisis point for me in midlife. Reflecting on life, debt and divorce from this more mature season, I imagine my young soul concluding that money mattered more to Mom and Dad than I did. The family focus on finances must have convinced my formative self that I was not important enough to deserve adult attention. Inwardly permeated by parental shame I came to believe that I was unworthy, too.

31

The message received was that I must be a quiet, good child because adults have more important things to do than notice me. My mission was to intuit what others needed and to do whatever I could to help them get it. Love and money got all mixed up for me. Eventually I forgot my own wants and needs. My path became "*Go along to get along*" which lead me in and out of financially-fraught marriages in the valley of the shadow of debt.

FIRE: THE THIRD ELEMENT
UNCHECKED DESIRE: A TRUE CRIME STORY

We are what we think. Speak or act with an impure mind
and trouble will follow you. Buddha

Judy is twelve when the first Fred Meyer Store opens on Hawthorne Boulevard in Portland. Attracted to the Grand Opening, just a fifteen-minute walk from home, she strolls alone through the wide department store aisles. Shelves are piled with attractive items. Judy has fifty cents in the pocket of her pedal pushers. Baby-sitters earn just twenty-five cents an hour in 1952. She can't afford to buy much of anything but an elegant fountain pen fires her desire to acquire. The pen, maroon with gold trim, inflames her imagination. Judy picks it up, enjoys its heft and balance. She puts it down, torn between how little money she has and how big the price on this lovely fountain pen. When a tiny bottle of green ink catches her attention, desire increases as Judy imagines how lovely her story of jungle girl and monkey will look copied onto the page in emerald letters.

An observant child, Judy notices that cash registers are far apart and that sales clerks are chatting among themselves. She notices how little attention they seem to be paying to her. This girl has learned the art of making herself invisible to avoid irritating her short-tempered father. She tries it here and confirms that nobody is watching. Pushing her glasses up on her nose, she glances out from under long brown bangs, checking to see that none of the adults are glancing in her directions. An innocent demeanor comes naturally to Judy. She is, after all, a good girl.

One hand casually resting in a pocket, she picks things up and puts them back on the shelves. Ready to risk, Judy casually palms the gold-trimmed fountain pen, transferring it from right hand to left and slipping it silently into her pocket. That was easy. Feeling bolder, she moves along the aisle, picks up the bottle of emerald green ink and smoothly transfers it to her other pocket. Folding hands around her loot, moving silently on soft-soled sneakers she strolls out the wide glass door and crosses the busy street.

Judy pauses beneath the marquee of the Baghdad Theatre, pretending to read movie posters although she cannot concentrate on Coming Attractions. Heart pounding, eyes angling out from under her bangs, the girl's attention is fixed on the store exit. Is anyone pursuing her? Did any of the clerks notice her small theft? Wow, it looks like she's in the clear. As the fear of being apprehended for theft diminishes, the thrill of getting away with it increases. Causally Judy strolls down 38th Street until Fred Meyers is out of sight. Then she skips giddily, heading home with stolen pen and ink in hand and a shoplifter's secret tucked into a corner of her crooked little heart.

MY STORY AS TOLD BY STUFF:
THE POVERTY OF ABUNDANCE:

Bread machine.
    Deep-fat fryer.
        Ice-cream maker.
            Electric foot massager.
                Curling iron.
                    Waterbed.
Travel trailer.
    Mercedes Benz.
    Sailboat.
        Hot air balloon.

Like many women who came of age in the 1950s I bought into the idea that the more labor-saving gadgets I owned the better life would be. Anyone who has actually cleaned a deep-fat fryer after one failed attempt at homemade donuts knows better. The fabulous things I wanted soon became redundant, redolent with post-purchase melancholy. Nearly every item I bought to make life more varied and more interesting has, in the long run, had the opposite effect.

In the 1980's my friend Penny invited me to join a small group to focus on money, to help each other grow up financially. Six women committed to study, pray and count every penny we earned, spent, saved or gave. We met twice a month, working our way through mimeographed work sheets and audio tapes created by Vicki Robin and Joe Dominguez. Founders of The New Road Map Foundation, they resided in one house with nine adults, pooled their earnings, kept costs low and paid the bills by leading workshops titled "Your Money or Your Life." Their worksheets linked faithful intention with fiscal attention.

We women told our truths and listened with mercy, reporting failures and successes at tracking income and outgo. We uncovered blind spots and confessed discrepancies between what we said and what we actually did with our money. We burned away fiscal illusions and delusions, gaining financial and emotional maturity. Growing in clarity and power led each woman to leave her job in San Francisco and move on to love and serve in more authentic ways. Exploring money difficulties, delights, discoveries and dynamics is a combustive combination.

The good news is that this beloved community set me on the path toward financial freedom. The bad news is that my cupboards and closets still kept filling up. I refused to rent a storage locker. Accumulate or eliminate, that is the question. Seeking ways to simplify led to The Absence Test devised by London executive Jeremy Bullmore: *How much would I miss this item in a crisis?*

Today as I write, ash from nearby wildfires sifts down on my Southern California roof. If ordered to evacuate, how much would I miss this mirror or that vase, this book or that lamp? On a scale of 1 to 100, how vital would this be in a fire, flood or earthquake? Bare necessities and simple pleasures rarely disappoint. Still, stuff tends to pile up. When do I accumulate and when do I eliminate? Once a year I apply The Usefulness Factor:

Have I worn this jacket within the past year?
No? OK, out it goes to someone who needs a jacket.
Have I baked any food in this Pyrex dish during the year?
Nope. Off it goes to the community rummage sale.
Am I likely to use my cross-country skis, poles and boots within the next year? Here's where honesty and fantasy arm-wrestle.
No, I haven't gone cross-country skiing for five years.
Yes, I have fudged on the annual review a few times.
OK. Sigh.
It really is time to give away my favorite ski stuff. I can always rent equipment if I want to go cross-country skiing some fine winter day.

I haven't been backpacking lately, either, but I'm not ready to let go of the hope that I might. Not yet. Sometimes I bend my own Usefulness rule. This year I tuck my backpack gear back into the closet. I might still hit the trail some day. God only knows…

BREAD: THE FOURTH ELEMENT
TASTE THE BREAD: THE JOY OF EATING

Man does not live by bread alone. Every now and then he needs a cookie.   Groucho Marx

Does any human activity, lovemaking aside, bring more pleasure than eating? My brother Jim thought so. When esophageal cancer reduced his appetite and destroyed his capacity to taste food, Jim seemed to lose interest in going on. *"Why live when I can't enjoy eating?"* he concluded. Once food lost its savor my brother declined a second helping of chemotherapy. He died midway through his sixty-second year—too young, far too young. I miss him.

My family loved to eat. As children we heard Bible stories about slaves escaping Pharaoh's whip, sad to miss the good old foods from the old days of bondage. Men complained about the strange stuff called manna. Women lamented as they struggled to find water for their families. My people in Oregon endured no such hardships. Water was plentiful and food was ample. Men and boys fished the rivers, dug oysters from the sand, hauled up crab from the sea and stocked the freezer with venison, trout and salmon. Women and girls picked berries and green beans from farm fields and plucked ripe fruit from friends' orchards. We worked together peeling peaches and pears, canning apricots and applesauce, lining basement shelves with jars of summer food to enjoy during winter rains. As Erma Bombeck put it, *"I come from a home where gravy is a beverage."*

I took bread and gravy for granted until my first trip of perspective to Haiti in 1990. Poor peasants opened their huts to our little band of privileged Americans. We ate rice and beans cooked over charcoal fires, slept on the ground atop piles of clothing and bathed in shallow plastic basins in water carried by girls with buckets on their heads. We visited Creole literacy centers and listened to struggling members of peasant cooperatives. We helped Missionary Sisters of Charity tend to babies abandoned by mothers who could not feed them. We bathed bony bodies of women with AIDS and changed bandages of men wounded in street violence.

"Cooked food has no owner." The truth of this Creole proverb became evident during a meal hosted by Haitian activists. Guests and hosts sat together under a carob tree singing, playing with the kids and talking of socio-economic political tensions. When invited indoors to fill our plates I politely spooned up small portions from the cooking pots. I later found them empty when I went back for a second helping. The reason was visible. A dozen neighbors sat in the shade eating with gusto. Drawn by the scent of rice and fish sauce, folks brought bowls and quietly helped themselves. Cooked food belongs to the community in Haiti.

Food shock hit when I returned home from the poorest nation in the hemisphere to shop the overstocked shelves of my supermarket. With new eyes I saw a plethora of produce, cereals, cans, meats and packaged goods. Stunned by stacks of bagged pet food, I stood stock-still in the aisle, painfully aware that Haitian people have fewer food choices than American pets.

During a courtship dinner decades later, my beloved and I were telling each other about unforgettable meals in the course of our individual lives. Pete had served as a Navy medic and a teacher abroad and enjoyed the foods of many continents. After I described this Haitian meal as memorable, Pete asked:

> *What made it special?*
>> *Was the aroma of Jesus present there?*
>>> *Could it have been the Bread of Life that made this meal so memorable?*

Yes, that was it! A dear man who barely knew me listened with such care that he was aptly able to name an element that had eluded me. Such deep sensitivity is a pearl of great price. See why I married him?

WATER: THE FIFTH ELEMENT
SPENDING: KNOW THE FLOW
MY DYSLEXIC PATH TOWARD STEWARDSHIP

> *Like good stewards of the manifold grace of God, serve one another with whatever gift each of you has received.*
>> I Peter 4:10

I never won a game of Monopoly in my life. My brother Bob never lost one. He grew up to earn Certified Public Accountant credentials and be entrusted to invest university funds and family fortunes, which he did carefully and wisely. It seems to me that my CPA brother received more than his fair share of fiscal DNA. Bob is a whiz with numbers and I am definitely not. I earned As in college except for a D in Introduction to Economics. I simply could not master the concepts even though I had *"purchasing power."* Economic theory looks to me like a pirate ship far out at sea, glimpsed through fog. Concepts of wealth are equally elusive, like yachts that belong to someone else and never come close enough to touch. Fiscal dyslexia makes it hard to balance the checkbook let alone to comprehend the complexities of prime rates and globalization of trade.

God's gift to me is more soulful than financial yet I was well into my forties before it occurred to me to pray about money. Like many of you, perhaps, it was unthinkable to bring financial matters to God. Even after I began to notice discomforting connections between recurring financial struggles, my disappointing love life and my spiritual thirst, it still struck me as odd when my spiritual director suggested that I pray about money.

36

MEETING MY SEVEN DWARVES

With the gentle encouragement of my spiritual guide I began to get acquainted with my Seven Dwarves, the inner tag-team that toiled to keep economic confusion out of my awareness. *Graspy* was first to reveal her name. This hidden part of me felt such a lack of love and money that she held on too tight to whatever did come along. Other secret selves gradually came to light: *Sleepy*'s job was to snooze through inner conflict and act like everything would be fine in the morning.

Hi-ho, hi-ho, it's off to work we go chanted *Gloomy* and *Grumpy,* shouldering shovels and marching off when *Denial* and *Dorky* failed to keep financial problems buried in the unconscious. Eventually I even met *Sneaky*, the part of me who wouldn't openly acknowledge that she had any needs. During the child-raising years, for instance, *Sneaky* was part of me, as she had been since my shoplifting incident at age twelve. It was her influence that led me to conceal U-No candy bars in the freezer, inside an empty lima-bean box, so nobody would know that Mom kept a secret stash of sweets hidden from the kids.

I prayed about health, of course, and about relationships and vocation. I prayed for peace of mind but it had never occurred to me to seek God's guidance in money matters. I could hardly believe it when my dear spiritual director asked how I might take the Seven Dwarves into prayer. How humiliating. Didn't she get it? I could barely acknowledge their existence, let alone take such secrets to God. As if the Omniscient One didn't already know me inside and out...

Growing up without healthy models of economic and spiritual inter-dependence led me to invent a deadly pattern of *faux* independence. Each time I faced a tough financial decision I would swing from one extreme to the other, either obsessively calculating and refiguring the costs and benefits or impulsively spending or giving away too much. I hadn't had much fiscal autonomy as a daughter or as a wife. Now that I was single, I *liked* controlling my own money. I stubbornly refused to give up my purchasing power, even to God. I set my jaw and held onto the pretense of control for an embarrassingly long time, despite cycles of anxiety and stress under financial pressure. Could this be what the prophet Isaiah meant by a "stiff-necked people"?

PRAYING ABOUT MONEY

*The fruit of silence is prayer, the fruit of prayer is faith, the
fruit of faith is love and the fruit of love is silence.*

Mother Teresa

Taking money matters into prayer did not come naturally. The truth
is, I didn't really want to pray about my financial choices. Feeling safe with
a trusted spiritual guide freed me to become a little more honest with
myself. Deep down I had to admit that I was still mad at my parents for not
being more honest. They had spanked me for lying but hid their own lies
and secrets until long after I had made some fiscal whoppers of my own.
OK, my early training in money matters was insufficient. Some of it was
misguided and some was just plain wrong. So what? It is time to quit
blaming the folks, forgive them their debts and move on.

Gradually, given enough spiritual guidance and support, I was able
to stop hiding in the dark with seven thirsty dwarves. After a while I could
let *Sneaky* and her sisters drink deeply from the well of Love. Financial
and emotional freedom began to drench me too, true freedom to
acknowledge what I needed and to quench my thirst with Living Water.
Eventually, with divine assistance, I was able to relinquish the illusion of
control and to move past resistance to relief.

Now that my hair is turning gray I actually enjoy bringing money to
God. In prayer I usually get some kind of intuitive leading, a gut-sense of
rightness or wrongness about a particular financial choice. If I trust this
inner sense, even when it doesn't fit the advice of financial experts, things
seem to work out for the best. Whenever a clear sense of direction is
lacking I take that as a sign to wait in the light until clarity emerges. Prayer
has become the most natural way to link love and money. Steps include
naming what's real, noticing what's important, claiming Love's vision of
enough for all, making personal financial choices with care and reverently
savoring the results.

Read on to enjoy some true stories of past, present and future
stewards. These are my heroines, women and girls who know, show and go
with the holy flow, men who generously dedicate love and money to others
who need it.

SURPLUS: STEWARDING
INVESTMENTS THAT MAKE A DIFFERENCE

Thousands have lived without love, not one without water.
W.H. Auden

I had made a good start organizing my finances long before it occurred to me to write this guide. When one is fiscally dyslexic it is imperative to locate trustworthy financial guides. It took awhile to find the right match with the right financial professional. Once I found folks whose values matched mine I gained confidence in knowing the flow of my funds. I breathe freely now that my retirement account is under the care of faith-based financial professionals. Heart and mind, body and soul know that my wealth surplus is giving the working poor a chance to thrive. Retirement money is invested in a balanced portfolio of socially responsible investments (SRIs), community development financial institution funds (CDFIs) and OikoCredit, a global ecumenical *'bank for the poor"* modeled after the Grameen Bank of Bangladesh. "My" money flows to community cooperatives and micro-credit institutions such as Fonkoze in Haiti. My religious congregation, The Religious Society of Friends entrusts commonly-held funds in Friends Fiduciary Corporation, good stewards since 1898.

Got checking or savings accounts?
Purchase goods or services?
Own stocks or bonds?
Then you are an investor, too ...

During the civil rights movement African-American people began practicing socially responsible investing. Many folks chose to patronize African-American business owners and service providers. People of all ethnicities are putting their money where their values are these days through:
o   Consumer purchasing power
o   Shareholder advocacy
o   Screened stock investments
o   SRI money market and mutual funds
o   Community development credit unions and banks
o   Community investments in affordable housing
o   Community investments in small businesses
o   Community investments in land trusts

SOCIALLY RESPONSIBLE INVESTING:
SOME RELATIONAL RISKS

*The function of freedom is to free someone else. If you are
no longer wracked or in bondage to a person or a way of
life, tell your story. Risk freeing others.*   Toni Morrison

The move from habitual consuming to intentional simplifying has
been a bumpy process.   Seeds of simplicity weren't fertilized enough to
sprout during my first marriage but grew quickly in the early 1980s when I
sought guidance from members of The War Tax Resisters League.
Choosing to withhold ten per cent of my federal income tax assessment, a
symbolic tithe, from the military budget gained front-page media attention
and unwelcome attention from the IRS.   That furor calmed down after I
began serving city churches as part of an intentional ministry team and my
earned income fell below the federal poverty lines.

Writing a money autobiography turned out to be a powerful exercise
in self-awareness. I gained strength and support for change by participating
in workshops sponsored by *Ministry of Money* and by covenanting with a
small group of women to *"hear each other into speech."* Each step took
power from the demon of debt and bestowed it on the angel of surplus.
You, too, can try this at home by checking out Queries: Hearing Your Inner
Guide in Chapter Six and experimenting with writing your money
autobiography in Chapter Eleven.

Now: a caveat. Some of my choices and actions created distance
from some of my loved ones.   There's nothing like rocking the boat of
socially-held assumptions to make waves.   Habits of buying, having and
keeping money secrets go pretty deep.   Raising questions and changing
patterns separate me from some family and friends who merrily continue
acquiring, accumulating, cruising and boozing in pursuit of The Good Life.

Dedicating oneself to the seven-dimensional household covenant of
Sabbath Economics and to the five consciousness-lifting elements of The
Great Invitation can lead to lively engagement with like-minded others. It
can also lead to uneasy estrangement from differently-minded dear ones.
People who share similar values and commitments are good partners in
challenging injustice.   Financial conversion has personal risks, though.
Differences of opinion about money matters can lead to estrangement,
especially around traditional ways of celebrating Christmas, birthdays,
holidays and summer vacations. Becoming painfully aware of the planetary
and social costs of commercialization lead me to refrain from a lot of former
consumer-based pleasures. Choosing to save money and natural resources
has relational costs, less closeness with loved ones who enjoy the pastimes
and pleasures of the marketplace. Some of my dearest kinfolk revel in

technical gadgets, cars, clothes, home decor and tourism. I don't. Over time our common ground diminishes. Diverging views challenge family values, sometimes leading to relational difficulties and distance.

Co-leadingTrips of Perspective to Haiti in partnership with the founders of such non-profit ministries as *Journey Into Freedom* and *Beyond Borders* were truly transformative. These experiences went a long way toward freeing me from consumerism and forming me for stewardship.

SALT: THE SIXTH ELEMENT
NEIGHBORING: A CHILD'S STORY AS TOLD BY TRAUMA

Do I contradict myself?
Very well, then, I contradict myself.
I am large, I contain multitudes.

Walt Whitman

Good neighbors teach children what it means to be a good neighbor. When I was very young I had a sense of belonging and safety in one part of my neighborhood but a fearful wariness about venturing into another part. Not all neighbors are beneficent. It takes forever to heal wounds that some neighbors inflict on others. Telling the following story from the safe distance of a third-person perspective avoids rubbing salt into early wounds. The salt metaphor serves instead as a preservative, protecting the healing work of a lifetime in order to take adult risks with incarcerated neighbors.

Once upon a time there was a little blonde little girl named Judy Lee. She did not have a cape like Little Red Riding Hood but she was proud of her tall red rubber boots. Judy's mother was a good cook and a good neighbor. She often put bowls of warm food in her daughter's hands, zipped up the child's jacket and sent her down the street to Mr. Delaney's house. The old neighbor did not know how to cook and did not eat well since his wife had died. The child did not like going to the dirty, dark house of the dirty old man, but did as her mother bid.

One wet night Mr. Delaney grabbed her hair and pulled the child into his house. He held Judy Lee by the neck and pushed something stiff into her mouth. The old man's pants were down by his knees. Something smelly and salty filled the little girl's mouth. She fought for breath, struggling to not smother. Finally she broke free and burst out the front door. Dizzy and disoriented, she plunged off the edge of the porch and landed in a puddle. Gasping and spitting, Judy Lee rested her feverish face in the mud, too terrified to cry. Afraid that the nasty neighbor would come out and get her, Judy Lee picked her self up and sobbed her way home.

Neighbor and trauma joined hands when this little girl was only in kindergarten and held tight for a very long time.

You are the salt of the earth. But if the salt loses its saltiness,
how can it be made salty again?　　　　　Matthew 5:13

NEIGHBORING: PRISON SOLIDARITY
CONFESSIONS OF A FRIGHTENED WOMAN

"I was in prison and you did not visit me," Jesus said
　　　　　　　　　　　　　　　　　Matthew 25:43

But I'm too busy," said I. *Too judgmental. And too scared.* Then something happened. Love got my attention. The Alternatives to Violence Program salted my imagination during a difficult marriage. I found myself going through what I had witnessed long ago between my abusive grandfather and my patient grandmother. Intimate violence was wearing down my spirit. Hoping that better communication skills would make things better with my husband I signed up for AVP. Among a lively learning/serving community I found the kindness and respect missing at home　Although I was led to the Alternatives to Violence Project by personal reasons, something transpersonal transpired once I committed myself to completing three levels of training. I began to re-imagine nonviolence and to re-enact playful ways of interacting with others. The transformative process of AVP salted my readiness to connect with neighbors behind bars.

What might it be like to reach out beyond my sheltered life and actually venture behind the razor-wire?

What might I learn about loving self, God and others by interacting with tattooed felons?

Jesus invites privileged people like me to visit incarcerated neighbors who are deprived of the freedoms I take for granted. For sixty years I ignored this part of the gospel, an unwelcome challenge to my comforts, conveniences and choices. I was too frightened to visit prisoners until AVP training strengthened my willingness to risk it. The first step was small and personal. I simply began writing letters to a woman on Death Row. Rosie welcomed my letters and asked me to visit her. After months of paperwork and a five-hour drive to the remote prison she and I met in a locked glass-walled room. Gradually we grew to like and trust each other.

42

A friendship is born between a cautious grandmother and an incarcerated neighbor.

NBIs BEHIND BARS

The next step was to join an AVP team. I first volunteered to work with adolescent males in a youth correctional facility. That was more taxing than I had expected so I teamed with "inside facilitators" to introduce AVP principles and practices to adult convicts. To my surprise I discovered that my soul is nourished by regular participation in AVP. Saltiness means being more courageous and more outrageous, more willing to hear and follow inner guidance, more spontaneous in taking right action and more willing to give and receive larger helpings of loving-kindness.

Prison construction is booming. The Correctional Officers Union, already the largest and most powerful lobby in California, is growing faster than the Teachers Union. The suffering of crime victims and their families keeps increasing along with the anguish of inmates, their spouses and their children. Poverty, crime and punishment are intertwined. The contributions of convicted persons are lost to society. Some of us hear the cries of people who are enmeshed in the prison system, new truths from voices unheard in the free community. How to respond?

"Men in blue," as inmates like to be called, are hungry for healthy ways to interact with each other and with outsiders. They love having NBI's—*Never Been Incarcerated"*—outsiders come inside to share hidden truths, lively laughter and tender care. Prisoners support each other in practicing nonviolent communication. Everyone messes up; we all learn from our mistakes and encourage each other to risk new forms of imagination, compassion and effectiveness. Transforming Power surprises everyone when outbursts of grace take us beyond personal limits as we become catalysts for change. Imagination and interaction are re-activated. Fresh questions emerge:

What kind of spiritual practices lead ordinary women and men to befriend the strangers who are held captive by our society?

What can we learn from those who led the way, foremothers and forefathers who have shared the common lot of prisoners throughout history?

43

AIR: THE SEVENTH ELEMENT
EARTHCARE: RESTORING
REFLECTIONS ON BIOPHILIC MUTUALITY

*God is the source of being that underlies creation and
grounds its nature and future potential for continual
transformative renewal in biophilic mutuality.*
Rosemary Radford Ruether

Humans have always been story-tellers. Pondering what it means to be alive on earth at this time, wondering where God is amidst global warming, people create songs, poems and stories just as our ancestors did. Feminist theologian Rosemary Radford Ruether identifies three movements that happen before people get to the meaning-making called theology. First comes some sort of surprising direct experience with The Holy. Moved to respond, the next step is attempting to express the inexpressible by sighing or slumping, weeping or writing, singing or shouting, drawing or dancing. The third step is telling our story. Scriptures from all religious traditions are rich with stories of human encounters with Divine Power. Theologizing comes last. You and I may have stories about love and money that describe what happened around us and within us. Sorting out the meaning of these experiences is called theologizing. This may take some time.

In my process of theologizing about all this, Dr. Ruether's phrase *biophilic mutuality* strikes a resonant chord. I'm not sure I can define it but something about it shimmers. I breathe with it, holding *biophilic mutuality* in my mind and pondering it in my heart. After awhile body memories arise, mysterious long-ago experiences that seem to fit into the theological framework of an eco-feminist theologian. I trust Rosemary Radford Ruether so I invite her affectionate presence to join me in contemplation as I recall

❖ The evening I sat meditating on a rock at the edge of a lake in the Oregon Cascades....palms turned up, resting on my thighs ... face lifted to the sky... mind quiet ... breathing the cooling air. Something touched the center of my right hand. I enjoyed the sensation with a calm mind. It tickled a bit but I chose to keep eyes closed rather than look at what might be there. After awhile a matching tickle began in my left palm. Curiosity overcame caution. As my eyes flew open, two white moths lifted into the air, flying in unison into the sunset. *Biophilic mutuality?*   Maybe, but I'm not sure ...

❖ The hot summer day at Wellspring Renewal Center when a fly landed on my face while I sat with a group in prayer. I did resist the impulse to brush it away. Making a conscious choice to honor its presence, then intuiting the creature's thirst, quick tears formed and flowed. The fly drank at the corner of my eye, quenched its thirst and flew away. Aaah, .maybe that's what Rosemary means by *biophilic mutuality*...

❖ Another afternoon during Redwoods Summer, keeping vigil on a Mendocino County logging road with folks of faith, we heard the murderous whine of chain saws killing ancient redwoods . I saw tears leaking from the cut ends of majestic mother trees chained to the backs of logging trucks and heard the cries of daughter trees orphaned in the old grove.

❖ Yes, *biophilic mutuality* is more than a dry theological concept. My experiences are more than isolated incidents. They have more meaning than just interesting stories. Peculiar and puzzling as my cross-species experiences were at the time, Rosemary Ruether shows me how to honor these moments of oneness with moths, flies and trees when I became part of God's unity with nature.

❖ All this leads me to wonder if dogs and cats actually pray. If prayer involves reaching out in love, what about my grand-dogs Jezebel, Reba and Dante? How about the comforting presence of my grand-cats Apollo and Sebastian? Biophilic mutuality prompts me to re-examine some old anthropocentric attitudes. Would Creation limit prayer to *homo sapiens*?

❖ Next time I'm standing in the need of prayer I can imagine surrounding myself with a loving circle of grand-pets, enjoying and appreciating their care and comfort.

CHAPTER SIX
QUERIES: HEARING YOUR INNER GUIDE

Does this offend you?   John 6:61

The practice of posing pointed questions goes back to the Hebrew prophets. Jesus asked hard questions of everyone from power-brokers to poor peasants. Queries have been a central part of Quaker life since the 1600s, an evolving set of questions based on Friends' practices and testimonies which guide individuals and congregations in self-examination. They have often been helpful in evaluating my choices and actions, pointing the way for new growth. Good questions do raise awareness, clarify confusion, invite self-awareness and lift up social concerns. They can be uplifting and empowering, affirming my commitment to move forward with love and money. Queries can also create tension when I notice how far I am from living in accord with my own values. Hard questions lead to dynamic tension in my spiritual life. You and I can walk away from these tough questions or we can choose to walk along with them. This guide recommends strolling along with probing questions for awhile rather than hurrying into premature answers.

PAUSING WITH PRESENCE

This guide is totally convinced that being present to the Sacred is more vital than anything else when exploring delicate issues like love and money. Presence is more important than questioning. If one of the following queries makes you bark *"I don't know!"* it may be time to put down the book, pause, take a deep breath and notice what's happening in your body. Sensations such as tightness, jumpiness or itchiness may be signaling you to slow down and say hello to what is going on physically. Reframe a query as a suggestion, if that seems friendlier. For example, if a question like *"how much is enough?"* prompts you to growl *"I have no idea!"* then imagine someone gently inviting you to sense the quality of that growl, to listen for its inward message as a way of moving with it.

The path ahead is paved with queries. Some may poke or pinch. Some may hug or kiss. Stay alert. Some have your name on them and some don't. Approach each question with care. Embrace it if you dare. Bear it gently but persistently. Delve it with daring and deliberation. Keep one key question in mind: *Am I committed to seeing what love can do*? There will always be unanswered questions and room for growth. Allow unresolved questions and unsatisfied desires to take you where they will, maybe even deep to the core, to the dwelling place of your wise inner guide.

WHERE AM I NOW with the twenty questions that began this guide?
    What have I noticed about myself so far?
        What privileges and possibilities occur to me?

As I read the *Introduction—A Spiritual Guide*
    I notice the notions that rankled are …
        Which ideas resonated with mine?
            What put me off? Pulled me in?

What role do I see others playing in helping me discern my spiritual truth?
    Who assists me in financially figuring out how much is enough?
        What is the essential role of guidance for me?

What does "love" mean to me?
    How is love an active force in my community?
            How do I foster love in my extended family, neighborhood, workplace, congregation, on-line groups?

How would my life be different without love?
    How would my life be different without money?
        How does the love in my life relate to the economics of my life?

How much is enough?
    What does spiritual guidance offer me?
        What does love and money require of me?

What am I least grateful for in relationships today?
    What I am feeling most grateful about being, doing and having?
        What questions about love and money are occurring to me?

What were my very earliest associations with Spirit?
    What inherited beliefs went along with that?
        How did I relate to these beliefs?
            What came next?

How has my experience with religion shaped my soul?
            What event or issue prompted a shift from my early faith?
                How do I respond to those who claim to have The Truth?

How do I take a stand when I find what is true for me?
      Who or what points me toward the Eternal these days?
            How might I mend and tend my true heart's desire?

SABBATH SEED QUERIES   SLOWING

In which area of my life do I sense a "*flow*" between my efforts and Spirit?
      What happens physically when I'm "*in the flow*"?
            How does flow guide my thinking process?
            Affect my emotions?

What is Sabbath like for me these days?
      Which animals beckon me to slow down?
            Which plants invite me to pay attention?
            If I don't have real Sabbath time, how might I create it?

When I was young how did I spend unstructured time?
      How did family activities match my innate sense of the sacred?
            Tension between my ideas of The Holy and their ideas?

Looking back for my own early seeds of essence, what do I see?
      Who nurtured the seed potential within me?
            How did emptiness play into my coming of age?

How does religion shape my view of Sabbath—for better or for worse?
      How does scripture contribute to my perspective, ditto?
            How do earth, wind, fire and water restore my soul?

Where am I now on the continuum between Doing and Being?
      What happens when I encounter 'scary emptiness?'
            What sorts of accomplishments have a tight hold on me?

Looking back over my entire life, when was I most fragmented?
      When was I most happy and whole?
            What was my source of renewal then?   Now?

DEFICIT—LIGHT QUESTIONS   OWING

Through all the seasons of my life, where has debt taken me?
      What were the notable lows and highs of my financial life?
            When did hope arise amidst economic tempests and storms?

How has household deficit impacted my thoughts?   My feelings?
How does debt cause bodily strain or sickness?
What kind of life-giving energies emerge when I am able to
let go of what's not essential?

Which family deficits formed my views and values?
Where am I now on the debt/ freedom continuum?
Who is God for me when I don't have enough?

What was it like to go through the valley of the shadow of debt?
Has Spirit ever helped me move through a tough situation?
How did I act to take full advantage of spiritual help?

Do I recall any direct encounters with Light?
Did I make any deals with this mysterious Power?
Did I ever feel let down by God?

When did I become aware of learning something valuable from an older
person?
Have I ever been surprised to find myself in the role of guide to
someone else?
How has a child offered me a fresh perspective?

In workplace or congregation, do I have any idea of the burdens others
carry?
Is it OK to be aware of each others' financial troubles?
Do I acknowledge the essence of goodness in others that
wants to be recognized?

How do I see a written guide like this supporting my spiritual journey?
What parts might I risk sharing with family, friends, colleagues?
Where is electronic communication in money matters?

STUFF—FIRE QUESTIONS   SIMPLIFYING

Could I simplify my life in some of the ways I'm been reading about?
Do I even want to do anything different?
Do I know someone fiery enough to help me make changes?

What would happen to my identity if I didn't own certain brand items?
How can I let go of those cool things that define who I am?
How much spending and having is enough?

Have I ever heard an unexplainable voice in the past?
When? Where?
How did I open or prepare myself for that experience?

Do I recall a time when I received guidance from a source beyond myself?
Have I ever been prompted to give away some of my stuff?
Did this inner nudge come from a person or group?

How does my workplace or congregation oppose simplicity? Support it?
Do we know what makes each other laugh?
Do we know what others enjoy doing for free?

Do we know each other well enough to make valid assumptions about attitudes?
How often do we ask each other challenging questions?
Where might "How much is enough?" enter our dialogue?

FOOD: BREAD QUESTIONS   CHOOSING

Have I been pushing hard today? How does it affect my food choices?
What kind of energy am I bringing to today's meals?
Am I excited to gain sustenance and meaning?
Am I worn out, going thru the motions of eating?

Who and what shaped my personal views, values and ways of relating to food?
Did my family have ways of eating that I absolutely adore?
Does my body need more food or less now?
Am I a slow eater or a fast eater?
How do I feel about this?

In the past twenty-four hours did I eat more than is good for me? Less?
Am I addicted to chocolate, chips, ice cream or something else?
Do I beat myself up for eating what I think I *"shouldn't"*?
Do I graze constantly, or sit for meals?

When I'm feeling sick or weak, what foods to I instinctively seek out?
Which optimal foods rebuild strength and well-being for me?
What is my most challenging eating issue?

Have any recent events changed my habits and ideas about food?
Do I begin or end meals with a particular form of ritual?

How does eating help me cope with despair?   Desire?
What foods support me in maintaining a strong spiritual center?

Is there an approach to eating which I believe is mine to offer to others?
How does divine purpose strengthen me to follow this calling?
What is great about the way I choose to eat?
How might it be better?

What is it like when I eat with others? Is my critical voice loud or muted?
Do I wince when someone takes—or refuses—a big dessert?
Do I judge others for eating what I consider to be unhealthy,
ecologically unsound or politically incorrect foods?

Which spiritual practices, teachers and traditions are most nurturing?
How are my food choices fed by others?
How do I show respect for people who eat differently?

SURPLUS: WATER- FLOW QUESTIONS   GIVING

Do I hold money in checking or savings accounts?
Purchase goods or services?
Own stocks or bonds?
Think of myself as an investor?

How might Love be calling me into right relationship with money?
What does this years' tax return tell me?
What does next year's checkbook ask me?

How does my faith tradition guide my choices about saving?
How much does it encourage me to share with the needy?
Guide me in ways to cut my discretionary spending?
Choices about how and where to invest my surplus?

How might my surplus money foster freedom for others?
How can I invest time and tenderness on behalf of those in
economic bondage?
How might my congregation become better attuned to how
and where to corporately invest our common surplus?

In the past week, when and how was I a good steward?
How might I celebrate this free flow?
When was I least generous?

How might I mend these missed opportunities?
How much stewardship is enough?

NEIGHBORING: SALT QUESTIONS   BELONGING

When did I feel least connected today? Most connected?
Laughter and play brings me closer to others when …
Being with others replenishes my energy when…

How much of my treasure is invested where my heart is?
How about my *talent?*
Where do I invest my *time?*
How widely do I direct my *tenderness?*

Whose values and choices do I admire?
Whose service-oriented story appeals to me?
How might I learn more about getting involved?

How am I currently answering the call to generosity?
Whose unmet needs touch me most deeply?
How has my community service changed over time?

Supporting someone who was going through a disastrous time, I offered…
Recalling an instance of 'being in the present"
Remembering when time seemed to stand still…
Or a time when I failed to stay in the moment?

How is Spirit nudging me to connect with nearby neighbors?
Distant ones?
How do I relate with people who are quite different?
When have I shown love or shared money with
these neighbors?

How might I deepen and extend right relationship with people on the
margins?
Which of my spiritual connections benefit all neighborhoods?
How much commitment is enough?

52

When and where did I feel most drained this week?
>Where in the world do I recall feeling most vibrantly alive?
>>Another place that most expands my sense of Presence is...

When I listen to my deepest spiritual knowing, what do I long for?
>How do I act on these longings?
>>Desire to deepen my care for Earth expresses itself in...

A time in nature which moved me so deeply that it left a lasting impression...
>A moment when I experienced awe so deep that it stays with me....
>>Being "carried" through disaster or stress was like...

What troubles me most about predictions of a global eco-crisis?
>Something missing in my current approach to earth restoration is...
>>A nudge or leading I'm beginning to notice is ...

Where in the world did I felt most fragmented?   Most whole?
>How might my ways of using time and money contribute to both?
>>How might Spirit be calling me toward deeper unity with creation?

Would I do more for the earth if I did less for my own comfort and convenience?
>Who inspires me to become more invested in a restoration project?
>>How much involvement is enough?

CHAPTER SEVEN
RELATIONAL WAYS OF MAKING LOVE WITH MONEY

SABBATH PLAY
LOIS OF LONDON   SCULPTING WITH WHIMSY

Sculptor Lois Walpole combines Sabbath play with artistry, inventively weaving baskets from willow branches and recycled stuff including colourful strapping tapes, juice cartons, bottle tops, fruit nets and bright plastic bags.

Lois creates new art forms in new ways from new materials, each one unique. Experimenting with wires from champagne bottles, for example, she plays with each new material like a child, finding out what it will do and trying things out. Creating wildly imaginative laundry baskets since the early 1980s, Lois uses left-over textiles, wire, cardboard and orange-juice cartons for practical and beautiful forms.

As people keep bringing her more and more material to recycle into baskets, Lois affirms the necessity of creating a boundary. The artist honors the fullness of time through Sabbath attentiveness. She creates the fullness of shape in her basketry by focusing on making shapes of *"fullnesses and roundednesses."* Sabbath time is focus time for this artist. She trusts that not everything under the sun is known. Sabbath play inspires her to create new methods of construction with vibrant recycled plastics, designing repetitive harmonies offset by bold blocks of color. *"Visual jazz"* is the way ceramicist Sandy Brown describes Lois Walpole's contemporary basketry.

STUFF: SIMPLIFYING
SHOPOCALYPSE NOW   WHAT WOULD JESUS BUY?

If you want to know the power of the demonic try not being a consumer.
Stanley Hauerwas

Bill Talen, an anti-consumer activist, conveys the gospel of Shopocalypse through comedy instead of stern sermons. Founder of *The Church of Stop Shopping* Bill and a 35-member choir counter the forces of consumerism through street theatre. The *Shopocalypse Tour* was banned from all Starbucks coffee shops in California for distracting customers from their lattes, and services conducted by members of *The Church of Stop Shopping* have been banned from shopping malls across the land. On Christmas Day Reverend Billy and choir were escorted out of Disneyland for singing *"Our main streets are empty! Everything is outsourced! It's all made in China! Take the magic back, America!.*

Using street theatre to promote economic change, *The Shopocalypse Tour* claims three modest goals:

> *Convincing people to shop in ways that support the local economy*
>> *Encouraging businesses to be good for workers and not just for corporate shareholders*
>>> *Insuring just treatment of workers around the world*

STUFF: SIMPLIFYING
NANCY GOES SHOPPING   BUDDHIST FIRE

Nancy talked excitedly about a course in Greed Management she'd taken with The Buddhist Peace Fellowship. The *'final exam'* was the best part, she said. The point was to practice mindfulness in the midst of a busy retail environment. Everyone met at the Bed, Bath and Beyond store for a walking meditation through the aisles. *"It was undoubtedly the most unique shopping experience I've ever had,"* said Nancy.

"First I found the fluorescent lights and loud music annoying. After awhile it seemed like I was in a toxic atmosphere, at least that's how it felt to me. I had a little headache to begin with and it got worse the longer I stayed in the store.   I felt inundated by the sounds and smells. When I actually paid attention with all my senses, I noticed how scented the candles are, how textured the bathmats feel and how quickly I became overwhelmed. That was the point, I guess.   Stores are designed to seduce you with excess."

"Pondering whether or not I am greedier than someone else is pretty much beside the point," Nancy concluded. *"I quickly learned that in order to grapple with the vast subject of greed first I must examine certain details with care."*

To try this yourself, check out Spiritual Practices in Chapter Ten.

FOOD: CHOOSING
JEAN OF RAMALLAH   PALESTINIAN BREAD

"When I teach Home Economics" writes Jean Zaru, *"I ask eleventh and twelfth grade girls to describe how they will plan meals, buy clothes and run a household. This focuses on what it means to live responsibly in the wider Palestinian community.   What we buy and eat is important. Starting our meals from scratch is not only healthier and cheaper, but by buying local products, we help the simple farmer to stay on the land and not*

move to the city. We avoid the problems of waste or preservatives in processed foods. We avoid using products made by Israel, which are highly taxed. We cannot pray for peace and pay for war. The same is true with clothes. Why buy ready-made clothes when we have wonderful dressmakers, when we have women who knit at home for a living? We have to support them. All this may not bring about overnight change, but it empowers my students. It gives them a sense of worth and dignity. Their lives and choices count and so do the lives and choices of other women."

"For forty years I have been walking that edge where the spiritual meets the political. For me, the two have always been integrated. My faith as a Quaker Palestinian Christian woman is rooted in the human dignity and human rights of all people, and the sacredness of Mother Earth. I feel compelled to work for a world in which human freedom and dignity can flourish. Spirituality brings life and vibrancy and imagination to my struggle, but of course I recognize that the mixture of religion and politics can also fuel the most extreme and violent acts can lead to systems of self-righteous repression."

"Many activists mistrust religion and spirituality, sometimes for good reason. But each of us finds ourselves engaged in the work for peace and justice because something is sacred to us—so sacred that it means more than convenience or comfort. It might be God, or the Spirit, or the sacredness of life or belief in freedom. Whatever it is, it nurtures us."

SURPLUS: GIVING LIKE WATER
MARNI and BERNI of LOS ANGELES:
OLD MOVIES ARE GOOD MEDICINE

Steward   n: *A person who manages another's property, money, or other affairs.*
The American Heritage Dictionary

When they realized how easily they could live without all their favorite DVDs, elementary-school sisters Marni and Berni Barta decided to entertain hospitalized children with movies. Their volunteer work as good stewards began after a flood damaged the family home. For fourteen months the girls' stuff gathered dust in a storage unit while the house underwent repair. They began to realize how little they missed formerly favorite Disney films and Wee Sing musicales. Then their friend Alex developed leukemia. Watching movies from his hospital bed made Alex feel a little better. An idea was born. The girls loaded up a hundred of their own videos and DVDs and donated everything to the pediatric oncology department of Cedars-Sinai Hospital. *"Once you turn on a movie they like, it really soothes the children,*" said the nursing director. *"Films bring normalcy to their environment."*

Enthralled that their simple idea made such a difference to so many sick kids, the sisters asked friends and neighbors to donate their stashes of old movies. They contacted movie studios and production companies, got generous donations and sent films to hospitals around the country. For six years Berni, now 17 and Marni, now 15, have been gathering old movies to delight hospitalized children. Four movements summarize the girls' growth from entertainment consumers to non-profit service agency founders:

1- Flood, displacement and homecoming alerted the children to what was really important and what was extra.
2- Alex's illness touched their hearts and moved them to act, then patients, parents and nurses affirmed their generosity.
3- Friends, strangers and MGM donated thousands of films.
4- When pediatric units in LA-area hospitals had enough DVDs the girls held bake sales, raised money and shipped 28,700 movies to 287 hospitals as far away as South Africa.

NEIGHBORING: SALTY CHOICES
    BETH of DETROIT: LOVE THY NEIGHBOR

When she moved to an inner city neighborhood Beth embraced everything about urban life except the guys who ran the tattoo parlor on her block. The young women felt intimidated every time she encountered a shoving match on the sidewalk and resented so much yelling and punching in public space. Eventually Beth decided to get her own tattoo. She walked across and told the guys she wanted "Love thy neighbor" inscribed on her wrist. Beth explained that she was having trouble loving her neighbors because they were so rude and rough. She heard one tattoo artist say to the proprietor, *"Manuel, dude, we're scaring our neighbors. We got to stop fighting."*

After that the men calmed down and stopped fighting in public. Beth felt safer in her neighborhood. A few weeks later she ran into Manuel on the street. He surprised her by giving her a big hug and saying to his friend *"See, this here is my neighbor. She's the one I was telling you about."*

ELISABET' of PERU: IMAGINAL CELLS

What kind of butterfly might emerge from this mess?
                                                                    Lynne Twist

Evolutionary biologist Elisabet Sahtouris, a Greek-American now living in Peru, was the first scientist to identify *imaginal cells,* the mysterious collaborative force that converts common caterpillars into beautiful butterflies. The scientist's discoveries are thrilling on their own merit and also offer a powerful metaphor for a way humans might transcend the problem of economic excess.

Dr. Sahtouris' research focused on caterpillars at the point in the lifecycle where they become voracious gluttons, eating hundreds of times their own weight each day. The more they consume, the fatter and more sluggish they become. During this period of developmental excess the rare and scattered imaginal cells begin to stir deep within each creature. These minority cells are specifically designed as genetic specialists in transformation. When caterpillars are small, imaginal cells are few and far between but as the worms grow, so do the transformative cells. Eventually these far-flung imaginal cells find each other and join together to do their creative work as genetic co-directors of metamorphosis.

It is only during the feeding-frenzy stage that the mysterious imaginal cells connect and conspire.   When the over-consumptive caterpillar can eat no more, the transformative cells signal that the time has come for deconstruction.   At this point the bloated creatures dissolve into a mushy substance.   Out of this mucky nutritive soup the genetic directors create the miracle of butterfly.   It is a fitting parable for our time, both a metaphor for the greed driving our economy and destroying our planet and a word of hope for an emergent outcome.

In this world of turmoil and conflict, violence and retribution, I believe there are millions of people taking responsibility not just for change, but also for transformation. We may be in the minority, but we are everywhere and we are connecting with one another ...we are the genetic directors of this living system.
                                                                    Lynne Twist

CHAPTER EIGHT
SCRIPTURE: INVITATION and PROVOCATION

The truth of scripture is not about literal words, things and concepts. The truth of scripture is about relationships— relationships between God and us and between us as persons.
Jean Zaru

WRESTLING WITH LOVE, MONEY and SCRIPTURE

Some people are repelled by The Holy Bible, finding it too archaic and too patriarchal. Some folks object to ancient images of God as Lord, King and Judge. Others are attracted to scripture, finding assurance and affirmation in its pages, rejoicing in biblical images of God as Creator, Christ and Holy Spirit. Both groups tend to be perplexed by the views of the other, which can lead to judgmental ideas and critical feelings toward those who see scripture differently. Your own interest in the Bible may be salted with wariness. It is natural to wonder what dusty old words have to do with fresh new choices. What could the Bible possibly have to say about today's challenges with love and money?

A MIXED BIBLICAL BAG

The Bible is familiar.
Life is strange.
We bring the two together
To shed light on life.
Avivah Gottlieb Zornberg

Some aspects of The Holy Bible are confusing and some are clarifying. Some parts are timely, addressing specific conditions at certain times of history. Others are timeless, living words carrying meaning across eons. Psalms and parables are truly timeless Poetic Psalms and passionate parables form a double rainbow in my mind's eye, lighting human concerns with holy radiance and prismatic color. The beauty stretches from age to age, illuminating mundane affairs with sacred wonder. Praying The Psalms can lead to awesome encounters with the Divine Author behind the text. May Sabbath Economics and scripture shine with double radiance whether you are at the cautious end of the scriptural spectrum or at the carefree end of the rainbow. As poet Galway Kinnell muses: *Could it be that I am the pot of gold?*

START WITH LOVE

Love offers a starting place for biblically cautious people to engage with scriptural enthusiasts. Sabbath Economics provides common ground for people of all biblical opinions. You, the person holding this, I imagine you've had some encounters with love and a variety of experiences with money. You may have direct experience with the Holy and you may be hungry for more. Stay tuned—Sabbath practices suggested in upcoming chapters may intrigue and entice you.

You and I come equipped with unique expressions of body and soul, heart and mind, will and strength. As humans imbued with individual strengths and limits, we naturally tend to develop more fully in some aspects and give less attention to others. For instance, she may tend to focus on feelings more than theories while he may trust ideas more than sensations. Love asks us to respect and nurture ALL capacities, ours and theirs.

> *You shall love the Lord your God with all your heart, and with all your soul, and with all your strength, and with all your mind; and your neighbor as yourself.*　　Luke 10:27

"*Gospel*" means "*good news.*" Sabbath Economics links the good news of the great invitation to lure us toward wholeness. When spiritual and material matters unite, it seems more OK to bring money matters to prayer. Love for self, God and neighbor can ease itchy issues like debt, surplus and neighboring. For those with eyes to see and ears to hear scripture can nourish emotions and open the soul to deeper stirrings.

Bible passages can be dense as six-grain bread, laden with meaning beyond content, seeded with divine possibilities. Psalms and parables are especially invitational and transformational for 21st century folks. The ancient poems of The Psalter reflect the rawness of life as it was centuries ago and is today. People in many moods and different conditions addressed God in poetic prayers of thanks, praise, pain and lament. The Psalms are salted with feelings and seeded with sensations that nourish body and soul.

Parables offer food for the mind. Stories and similes told by Jesus 2,000 years ago were so memorable that disciples remembered and recorded them long after the end of their Teacher's life on earth. Short punchy parables stretch human concepts, stir the imagination, confound what we think we know and expand our minds to grapple with layers of spiritual and social meaning.

Pairing parables with Sabbath Economics directs us toward spiritual and fiscal maturity. As you and I honestly face our issues with accumulating, spending and debting, we grow up emotionally and financially. We become more aware, more able to use our personal and monetary resources in service to neighbors and Earth. Sabbath Economics offers powerful tools for the evolution of the human species and the transformation of the cosmos.

SABBATH: SLOWING
  SEED AS TRANSFORMATIONAL ELEMENT
    AN EGYPTIAN AHA!

> *This is what the Kingdom of God is like. A man scatters seed on the ground. Night and day, whether he sleeps or gets up, the seed sprouts and grows, though he does not know how.*   Mark 4:26-27

Seeds   are astonishing. How can so much come from so little, so quietly? Once upon a visit to the National Museum in Cairo, dazzled by the glare of gold and gems unearthed from King Tut's tomb, my eyes came to rest on a modest glass case. Seeds of varied sizes and shapes rested in a sectioned wooden box. Egyptian biologists planted some in a patch of dirt and watched to see what would happen with such ancient seeds. They rejoiced in awe when sprouts came forth from seeds hidden in a dark tomb for thousands of years.

SINK DOWN TO THE SEED

If seeds can remain dormant for millennia and still retain life, what about the seed of God in each person? Isaac Penington, a sixteenth-century Quaker mystic pondered this profound mystery and advised:

> *Give over thine own willing, give over thine own running, give over thine own desiring to know or be anything and sink down to the seed which God sows in the heart. Let that seed grow in thee, and be in thee and breathe in thee, and act in thee, and thou shalt find by sweet experience that the Lord knows that and loves that and it will seed thine inheritance.*

Jesus saw the seed of God in people and called it forth, revealing holy presence and purpose at work in everyday lives. Check out the parable of the mustard seed in Mark 4:30-32, Matthew 13:31-32, Luke 13:18-19 and Thomas 21. *"Sinking down to the seed"* means slowing down, savoring the sweetness of Sabbath and tasting the goodness and mercy of Living Love for your self.

DEFICIT: OWING   LIGHT AS TRANSFORMATIVE ELEMENT
    REFLECTION ON LOVE and DEBT

> *Love...with all your passion and prayer and intelligence and*
> *energy ...And love others as well as you love yourself.*
> Mark 12:30-31, The Message

Financial and emotional deficits are twin chains of bondage but freedom shines through Bible passages like a searchlight. Debt enslaves. Each person, created in the image and likeness of God, is designed to love and serve freely, in our own unique way, not bound by precedents set by patriarchs or prophets. This generation has been granted great spiritual options. We are free to link love and money in choices we make about owing, owning, spending, keeping, tithing, serving, giving, investing, neighboring and greening.

A Sabbath Economics covenant requires a high commitment. It goes beyond what peers may be willing to venture. Our range of freedoms has no script, no one-fits-all pattern. You and I may work out very different relationships with love, money, faith and practice. Then, and only then, can we extend what we've learned to our families, colleagues and congregations. Fiscal freedom will look different to each of us, defined by our own gifts and limits, within our own communities.

> *Then you will know the truth, and the truth will set you free...so if*
> *Love sets you free, you will be free indeed.*   John 8:32 NIV

DEBT: OWING   LIGHT AS TRANSFORMATIVE ELEMENT
    WHO IS GOD IN DEFICIT?

> *"Debt asks us to depart from the closely managed world of*
> *public survival and to move into the open, frightening,*
> *healing world of speech with the Holy One."*
> Walter Brueggemann

Scripture is filled with agonizing, life-threatening deficits that disrupted livelihoods, dislocated families and drove the people to the edge of survival. Jesus lived during an era of devastating hardship. Peasants he knew were doubly impoverished, forced to pay taxes and tolls levied by Roman occupiers as well as temple tithes levied by local priests. As biblical scholar Walter Brueggeman says, extreme conditions have always made people *"peculiarly open to the Holy One."*.

Where is God when deficit drives us to the edge of our capacity to cope?

More significantly, WHO is God when we suffer debt, despair and desolation?

Modern Jews and Christians inherited an ancient God of superiority and dominance. This is a Lord to be feared in patriarchal societies where the role of men is to rule and the role of women is to lament. Ancient kings claimed that their authority came directly from God Almighty. Royal power was diminished as it passed down the hierarchy from king to lord to vassal to serf. The idea of God as Lord led the ancient peoples to accept the divine right of kings. Dominating power profited a few and left the rest in debt. *"Absolutism was patriachy's handmaid and authoritarianism its stock in trade,"* concludes Benedictine Sister Joan Chittister.

In the Old Testament Book of Lamentations women cry out to an uncaring, unhearing Lord. Five poetic chapters of heart-breaking pain and loss convey the deep grief of women. Daughter Zion pleads for God's attention on behalf of destitute survivors in a city that has been destroyed, where sons have been murdered and daughters taken into slavery. Abandoned by a cruel, distant Lord, she laments with inconsolable widows, anguished mothers, babies dying at the breast and children begging for food in the streets. In contrast, the 23rd Psalm conveys the Lord as kindly shepherd, a God of goodness and mercy. What do we make of such contradictions? Can both God-images be equally true?

STUFF: SIMPLIFYING   FIRE AS TRANSFORMATIVE ELEMENT
        TO SHOP OR NOT TO SHOP?

If you want to change the world, who do you begin with, yourself or others?   Alexander Solzhenitsyn

What is the world, anyway? Solzhenitsyn defines it one way from his perspective as a Russian writer. Feminist biblical scholars envision the world as an earthly whole, seeing God as the divine Whole and persons as one-of-a-kind parts of the Whole. In their eyes the world encompasses everything within a universe of incomprehensible immensity, depth, beauty, divinity and sacred mystery. From this perspective the world is all of life—natural and political, scientific and economic, personal and public.

To shop or not to shop, that is the choice. But how in the world do you and I participate in changing the world, one choice at a time?

The Great Invitation offers a beginning point. Rabbi Jesus encourages us to develop ALL our capacities—brain, heart, gut and soul—and to love with ALL our faculties—thoughts, feelings, imagination, intuition and sensations. Sabbath Economics provides a method, encouraging us to bring all we've got—cognitive, emotional, intuitive and spiritual wisdom—into our private and public money matters. The more intentional we become in consulting the wisdom of our hearts and minds, bodies and souls, the more purposeful our choice-making can be and the more freedom we attain for ourselves and others. The Great Invitation and Sabbath Economic are powerful engines designed to boost consumers toward maturity, toward greater love in relational, spiritual and financial matters.

FOOD: CHOOSING   BREAD AS TRANSFORMATIONAL ELEMENT

How could you fail to perceive that I was not speaking about bread?   Matthew 16:11

Parables are bread for the brain. Imagine yourself holding three freshly-rising strands of bread dough. Inhale the yeasty fragrance. Enjoy the grainy texture as you braid the strands together into one loaf. The parables of Jesus join love, money and freedom into lovely loaves of challah. Braiding Sabbath practices with money matters with lifestyle choices lifts the loaf of our common life. Prayer suffuses money issues of deficit, saving, giving and investing with yeasty freedom. Tasty meditative practices infuse lifestyle choices of consuming, sharing and restoring with generous nourishment for self and neighbor. Enjoying yeasty Sabbath times nourishes us for greater study and service, transforming natural, material and spiritual conditions for many.

The Greek word *"para-bole,"* root of the word parable, means *"tossed near"* or *"put beside."* Jesus seemed to enjoy putting "this beside that" linking the kingdom of God with mustard seeds, for example, or tossing love and money together in the same story bowl. Mixing and matching metaphors opens space for multiple interpretations. Playing with metaphorical motions can spill over into *"a surplus of meaning,'"* provoking uneasy questions and stirring unexpected responses. This process can open minds, soften hearts and lift spirits.

Jesus seemed to enjoy mixing natural elements like light, water and breath into stories of social, personal and economic transformation. Putting *'this beside that'* gets a person thinking in new directions. You've probably noticed the synergistic spirit of this guide as we toss Sabbath Economic themes of deficit, consumption, surplus, sharing, solidarity and stewardship with spiritual elements of light, bread, salt, breath, seed, water and pearls.

In scripture the primal story of creation and sin centers on food. Plenty of fruit grows in the garden but man and woman want the forbidden fruit as well. Manna is a central theme of the Exodus when Yahweh discourages greed by providing no more and no less food than each family needs each day. The Bible refers to at least three kinds of hunger: common human hunger for daily bread, deep social hunger of famine and poverty, and spiritual hunger for God's presence. The three are connected.

> *"Blessed are those who hunger and thirst for righteousness,*
> *for they will be filled."*   Matthew 5:6

NEIGHBORING: BELONGING   SAVOR YOUR SALT
SIMPLE PRESENCE

He said "Bring me a new bowl and put salt in it."   2 Kings 2:20

Imagine each moment as a new bowl, empty and receptive to soul food. Imagine salt as a symbol of eternity, of the fullness of time. The emptiness of meditation bring past and present together in timeless peace. The *"peace that passes understanding"* can happen in an instant and last an eternity. The wordless depths of prayer can saturate people with a Presence that is both immense and intense. Spiritual practices help us notice, wonder, savor and respond to the taste of Presence. When we slow down and listen, we are free to receive. Each moment invites us into the More. And it is good. It is very good.

When we first get quiet, early fears and wounded feelings tend to get noisy and demand attention. Such inner clamor can be confusing when all we're trying to do is be still and listen for *"the still small voice."* Meditative practices can defuse powerful emotions like anger, guilt, shame and terror. *"Savoring your salt"* means getting in touch with what happened to you and within you, hard stuff that was very difficult to endure at the time. Persistence and courage are required in order to gain freedom with love and money. The bowl of prayer and the salt of eternity provide space and time to gather the spiritual gifts that outlast the old hurts.

IS IT TIME FOR AN ELEVENTH COMMANDMENT?

Comprehensive compassion is unfurling in the human species.   Brian Swimme

Quaker Earthcare Witness founders Ruah Swennerfelt and Louis Cox of Vermont found few answers when they searched Hebrew and Christian scriptures for guidance on how to live in right relationship with Earth. They found hints about being good stewards and passages praising the beauty and glory of creation but no warnings about the vulnerability of water, air or soil. Humans were not significantly altering the landscape at the time when the sacred scripture of most faith traditions were being written. Now our species is even changing the climate of the planet.

Members of The Religious Society of Friends trust that divine revelation continues, that new light is offered in each generation. For instance, slavery is not denounced in the Bible but Friends in colonial America came to a deeper appreciation of equality between humans. Concluding that slavery is immoral, Quakers gave up their slaves and eventually people of other faiths did the same. With greed, ignorance and technology-driven "progress" threatening to destroy the planet's fragile eco-system, Earthcare Witness asks if the time has come for an additional commandment. Do we need an eleventh commandment about being responsible, caring members of the entire family of life?

If Mother Earth hosted a reunion, how might our species unite to preserve the health of our eco-system so that all species could flourish? What might an eleventh commandment say about our spiritual relationship with our home planet?

CHAPTER NINE
BELOVED COMMUNITIES: COLLECTIVE CONVERSION

Good leadership comes from people who have penetrated their own inner darkness ... from people who can lead the rest of us to a place of "hidden wholeness" because they have been there and know the way."

Parker Palmer

JOURNEY INTO FREEDOM
DALE AND ESTHER of PORTLAND: LETTING GO

"Letting go is like releasing a tight spring at the core of your self, one you've spent your whole life winding and maintaining."   Sue Monk Kidd

Recently we, Esther and Dale, were moving one mile to a new home. As our "stuff" was being carefully and prayerfully transported, one friend asked "But is this all you have?" This surprised and amused us since we were feeling somewhat overwhelmed by all the boxes. We had just been thinking, "We have too much stuff." We were wondering aloud what the move would be like if we had followed in the steps of three of our many teachers:

Mother Teresa who owned only two saris and a bucket;
Sr. Jose Hobday who moved from Montana to California carrying all of her possessions in the back seat of her car;
A disabled friend who asked if we could help her move. Wondering how big a truck we would need to rent, we asked how much she had. She replied, "Two boxes and a TV set. Do you think that's too much?"

While we have less than in earlier periods of life, and have accumulated very little during the past decade, the truth is we have more than we need; more than we use; more than enough. Convinced that freedom and inner peace is about letting go, clear that letting go is at the heart of our faith tradition, certain that letting go is central to our call and ministry, it is also clear that neither one of us is very good at it.

Hard Work

Why is it so easy to accumulate and so hard to let go? Could it be that letting go, like compassion, forgiveness, and nonviolence is also an inside job? It seems true that our outward attachments reflect our inward attachments. We have discovered that until we are willing to let go of the stuff on the inside (i.e. our sense of privilege, our secrets, our right to have everything we want, our need to keep everything the way it has always been, our need for approval and control, our hold on people, our need to be significant, and our addictions, etc.), we are not ready to let go of our outward attachments to things, people, career, status, and stuff.

While letting go could be the greatest gift we can give God, ourselves, and others, it is also, without doubt, one of the most difficult and painful spiritual disciplines. The pain of letting go sometimes seems so unbearable that it is easy to understand why we put it off. Letting go is painful. Yet Jesus, Gandhi, Simone Weil, St. Francis of Assisi, the mystics, and other prophets testify that letting go of everything but God is a way to experience truth, love and freedom.

What We Mean by Letting Go.

The word "letting" means allowing, permitting. The word "go" means to leave, depart, exit, vanish, disappear, wither, fade. Together, the phrase suggests a kind of freedom that most of us claim we desire—but it tends to frighten most of us when we get close to letting go. For Esther and Dale, letting go means:

Being willing to be in the world without trying to own or hold onto the world
> *Having a non-possessive attitude toward everything and everyone*
>> *Having one goal: to hear what God wants in this present moment*
>>> *Embracing change, staying alert, standing with open hands and open heart to receive all gifts as blessings and grace;*
>>>> *Knowing that all accomplishments and works are products of the Spirit flowing through me;*
>>>>> *Focusing on the one thing necessary—an undivided heart.*

Where to Begin and How to Continue
Accept that relapse happens, that the journey is long, and the road is narrow.

Seek my truth. Work intentionally to break through my walls of denial about myself, my stuff, my communities, our nation and world.

Ask myself, in the safety of friends and community, some tougher questions:
What can I not walk away from both internally and externally?
What am I gaining by holding on, by not letting go?
What do I have that I don't need?
If I haven't used it in a year, who will I give it to?

Discern, with the help of wise mentors, my personal goals, mission and call. Clarity of call helps me detach from whatever blocks my way forward.

Practice the art of forgiveness daily. I am bound, and held in bondage, to those whom I have not forgiven.
Embrace and accept my imperfect self. I will always be a work in process.

Cultivate the discipline of centering prayer, which is both difficult and rewarding.
A friend's wisdom is helpful: "The goal of centering prayer, my dear, is not to have an empty heart or head, but rather to know what is in your heart and head and then let it go. Turn it over to God."

Let go of expectations about what might come next.
Letting go opens me to the unknown, engages me in the mystery.
Letting go opens up space.
And it is important to not fill up the space, the void created by letting go.

DEFICIT: OWING
BECKY and MARIAN of TORONTO:
TENDING and MENDING DEBT

Drawing Marian aside after Friends Meeting, Becky whispered *"I've heard the government can take your kids away when the heat gets turned off."* Marian reached out her hand to cover Becky's. *"Tell me what's happening."*

"Money has been tight for some time," Becky began. *"The prospect of another spare Christmas hurt, so I bought gifts for my kids on credit. When the bill came in January I paid it but when the gas bill arrived I couldn't pay that so I shoved it in a drawer without opening the envelope. I couldn't face the next month's heating bill either. Now I have a disconnection notice. The gas will be shut off on Tuesday."*

Marian realized that when a woman trusts you with her money troubles, she hands you a gift. Debt can create a bond that is both vulnerable and holy. When someone is in financial pain, it's best to reserve judgment and listen with empathy before trying to solve the problem. She may be blaming herself or expect to be blamed for her situation. Becky needs a listening ear. Laying down her burden to a kind listener might free her to take it up again a little more lightly.

Because of the urgency Marian acted alone at first and assisted Becky in contacting an energy assistance agency. She offered both a listening presence and a practical support. Then she called together a Quaker caring concerns committee. Several Friends met with Becky, supporting her in getting credit counseling and helping her make a long-term plan to reduce debts.

"Personal indebtedness is a place where Quaker concern for the simple life intersects with social justice," said Greg, a member of the care committee. *"I see Becky as a victim of economic injustice. Anyone carrying a balance of a thousand dollars on a credit card from month to month is in bondage to our consumption culture."*

"You've thought about this before," mused Adam.

"Yes, I filed for personal bankruptcy six years ago," said Greg.

"We never knew."

"That's the way I wanted it at the time," replied Greg. *"I was embarrassed and ashamed. Now I have a chance to help someone else by sharing some of what I learned."*

"Maybe it would be a good idea to offer an adult education program for the whole Friends Meeting," suggested Holly. *"I'm reading a book on voluntary simplicity and there are other Pendle Hill pamphlets on the subject. We can educate one another before we get into debt as well as afterward."*

The committee agreed that Becky's financial problems grew one choice at a time, leading to a crisis. Her situation prompted others to consider living more simply as a preventive action while addressing the spiritual condition underlying debt. *"At the same time, we want to be tender in talking about simplicity lest it prove a barrier to Friends who are carrying high debt loads. We don't want to risk any sense of shame about having made a mess of things,"* cautioned David. *"Exploring faith and finance is a first step, something we can do before people ask for help. 'The*

70

poor' are not just 'over there' but very near, among our own family, friends and neighbors." Love is the first motion. Friends wait and listen in the Light, seeking the guidance of Love in tending and mending lives torn by debt.

FOOD: CHOOSING
    ROB, IAN and DEAN of BOSTON:
      PUTTING MY MONEY WHERE MY MOUTH IS

We stand at a fork in the road.   Donald Altman

Rob, a lecturer at Yale, introduced the concept of commitment bonds as an incentive to overcome writer's block. He invited student writers facing deadlines to make out a check to him for a large amount, up to $10,000. Rob agreed to hold onto the check, return it if the writer finished work by the deadline or send it to a charity of his choice if they didn't. It worked: Rob never had to mail a check.

Ian, an economist, adapted the idea and made a weight-loss commitment contract with his colleague. He tells it this way: *I've had a lot of trouble keeping off excess weight. I'd lose dozens of pounds, but most of it would come back on within a year. Then I tried something new. I promised my co-worker Dean that I would lose 20 pounds and keep it off. I backed my intention by putting $500 at risk each week. If I failed to meet my goal weight, I owed Dean the money which he would then send to a charity of his choice. I lost 25 pounds and for the past 40 weeks my weight has remained remarkably constant. That's when Dean got serious about his own weight loss. Commitment bonds helped Dean lose 38 pounds. Neither of us has lost any money and our combined life expectancy has gone up by almost five years.*

As economists we're here to tell you that plain old-fashioned financial incentives—the risk of losing a substantial amount of money—is a pretty effective tool for change. In academic jargon, people often fall prey to 'dual-self models of temptation'. Odysseus had his crew tie his hands to the mast so he wouldn't give in to temptations of the sirens. Men today still need shipmates to make sure we don't succumb.

Ian Ayres and Dean Karlan launched a free internet service to help people stick to their resolutions. *"If putting up money is not for you,"* they say, *"put up your reputation instead. Post your goal and give us a list of friends. We'll tell them if you succeed or fail*

71

RUTHANN, JAN and LAILA of CHICAGO
      COOPERATIVE DINING: COOK ONCE, EAT ALL WEEK

When she opens the refrigerator after work, Jan and her children find three meals already assembled. Three friends have each agreed to prepare a single, large meal to feed each others' families. One goes into the cook's refrigerator. The rest is packaged up and exchanged on Sunday evenings. *"It's like eating at a restaurant, only you take what the chef has cooked,"* says Ruthann. *"When we get our meals, everything is in the bag including directions about how long it will take to cook or reheat."*

Cooperative cooking arrangements take many forms. The author of this guide gives away Sabbath Soup concocted each week from organic vegetables picked fresh at Farmer's Market each Sunday Laila organizes ten families in her neighborhood to cook and swap meals once a month. Ruthann and Jan belong to a 'pick-up' group of cooperative cooks who prepare and eat meals separately in their suburban homes. Potlucks and shared-meal groups thrive among residents of apartments, co-housing communities and college campuses across the country.

Cooking co-ops support healthy, green, economical food choices. Making one big meal for a crowd requires less money, planning and prep time than cooking five to seven meals for one's own family. Cooperative cooking minimizes the temptation to dine out or purchase expensive convenience or fast foods. Ethnic traditions are shared, inspiring participants to try out special recipes. And co-op cooking frees up the food budget to buy in bulk. Some groups accommodate vegetarians, some cater to self-identified *"foodies"* and others cook local, organic and/or vegan. Each form of cooperative cooking means that each cook spends less time shopping, preparing and cleaning up, and enjoys more time for talking, laughing and connecting over food with family and friends.

"Cooking co-ops are a perfect example of the ways that greening a whole category of our purchasing can work," says Alisa Gravitz, Co-op America's executive director. *"An organic, local apple may cost more than a conventionally grown apple, and Fair Trade Certified™ vanilla may cost a little bit more than conventional vanilla. But if you cook cooperatively, then the savings on your food budget from buying in bulk can make it possible to green your remaining food purchases. By thinking about the whole category of food holistically, you can eat greener, healthier, more varied meals—at the same cost as your old way of eating.*

LET IT FLOW
CHARLOTTE, BARBIE and MARY of PORTSMOUTH: STEWARDS of INHERITED WEALTH

To share often and much ... to know that even one life has breathed easier because you have lived, this is to have succeeded.

Ralph Waldo Emerson

Charlotte was born with the proverbial silver spoon yet she felt socially isolated as she was growing up. A large legacy freed her from the need to earn a living and freed her for the opportunity to grow spiritually. Charlotte studied, prayed and participated in money workshops, searching for ways to put her inherited wealth to work. She met Mary and Barbie whose hearts were also expanding. Linking love and money, the trio considered ways to encourage other women in following their own inner leadings.

The three Friends pooled their surplus wealth and began giving modest grants to support the spiritual journeys of women. They started small, keeping a low profile at first, inviting, interviewing and funding applicants they met through religious and personal networks. After seven years these good stewards were ready to legally incorporate the fund and go public. The grantors enlarged their community through annual gatherings to share spiritual practices with grantees. Mary died recently but Charlotte and Barbie continue to host annual gatherings, celebrative circles honoring the spiritual transformations funded by financial and prayerful surplus. They find stewardship of love and money very inspirational, more meaningful than other forms of philanthropy.

Six steps led these women toward dedicated stewardship:
1- Acknowledging discomfort with life in a society of wealth.
2- Committing to a path of intentional spiritual growth.
3- Connecting with women in circles of testing and trust.
4- Noticing 'nudges of the Spirit' and following one at a time.
5- Sharing their surplus first in a trickle then in a torrent.
6- Deepening relationships with grantees in mutual celebration

SHARING SALT
KRIS' STORY FROM HAITI:

You are the salt of the earth.

Matthew 5:13

In 1990 Dale Stitt invited me to get acquainted with Haitian neighbors in Port-au-Prince and on the impoverished island of LaGonave where families in the poorest nation of the western hemisphere struggle to survive. We befriended peasants, pastors and leaders of community co-ops, and continued to take small groups of privileged Americans to Haiti.

Soon after our group left the island nation, Haiti went through a violent period of political instability. The U.S. State Department advised Americans to get out. Volunteer teacher Kris Stoesz wanted to stay. She liked teaching at Matenwa Learning Center but she needed to know how her neighbors felt about having an American in the neighborhood during dangerous times. During a staff meeting Kris asked what they thought she should do. The room became still. One teacher said they would all understand if she wanted to go home to the States but it would make them really happy if she felt comfortable staying. Others said they couldn't predict how things would unfold but knew they would continue to teach the kids and to support one another.

"I was thrilled," Kris said, *"at how clear and easy their answer was. Then I began to notice that I was receiving more house visits from neighbor women. In Haiti it is typical to drop by each other's homes, but these visitors seemed more purposeful. Eventually I realized that these were visits of solidarity. People were coming by to make sure I wasn't sad or discouraged or too worried about the troubles.*

On February 27, 2004 a larger-than-usual group of neighbors arrived on her porch. *"We shared news of our families as usual,"* said Kris, *"but the mood was more somber. "* The island women had experienced times of violence. They reassured Kris that the shooting wouldn't reach their rural village but warned that everyone might get hungry if supply boats couldn't sail from Port-au-Prince. *"When one woman told me she was going to buy rock salt at the market, I responded that if we needed to start rationing food, salt wouldn't be the first thing I'd stock up on."* They glanced at one another and one neighbor said *"She doesn't get it."*

What's to get?

"Well," they repeated, *"rock salt is important when there's no food. If you have nothing to eat, your body systems shut down, and that's when you get sick. But if you put rock salt under your tongue it slowly dissolves*

and keeps the body going. My neighbors knew how to lessen the effects of hunger and wanted me to do the same. They were honoring me by teaching me how to live through famine, and by showing me how they support one another in difficult times."

Kris concludes: *"I did buy a little can of rock salt at market that day but the next morning we awoke to news that the president had left the country. For three days no food supplies reached the island of LaGonave then resumed after United Nations troops arrived. The rock salt remains on my shelf, reminding me of courageous neighbors and how we grow in solidarity through difficult times. Solutions aren't easy but we know we want to find them together. Neighboring may mean just listening, or learning unexpected uses for rock salt. Sometimes solidarity means living in close proximity, walking in one another's shoes and gaining new vision as we meet new challenges together."*

Kris Stoesz continues to volunteer with Beyond Borders, working for justice and peace by fostering transformative learning within and across cultural and economic borders.

NEIGHBORING   BELONGING
ELIZABETH of OLDE ENGLAND:
GIVING LOVE, MONEY, WILL and SPIRIT

Work is love made visible.   Ama Ata Aidoo

The image of Elizabeth Gurney Fry (1780-1845) appears on British five-pound notes today, a government tribute to a wealthy woman who tirelessly gave time, treasure and tenderness to clothe, feed and educate poor women incarcerated in London's filthy Newgate Prison. During the Vicitorian era she activated historic prison reform in two significant ways. Fry dedicated her own surplus of money, energy and compassion to women in need, and she encouraged wealthy Victorian women to leave the comfort of their drawing rooms and accompany her into dank dungeons to assist female felons.

How did one woman change the prison system? Elizabeth Fry's change of consciousness came first. Her call and commitment to stewardship stemmed from six spiritual practices:

1)   The presence and power of Quaker women sharing in circles of trust under-girded her lifelong public service.
2)   Silent communion with God led her to affirm *"Nothing short of the Holy Spirit can forward the cause of righteousness on earth, and therefore we desire to wait for its stirrings."*

3) Seeking to know and express the truth of her self, Elizabeth filled forty-six journals while coming to terms with her shadow and finding her way into the Light.

4) Queries were her daily bread, having inherited her questioning spirit from a long line of family and Friends.

5) She saw the seed of God in everyone, seeking the good in indigent children, inmates, wardens, magistrates, ship captains and members of The House of Lords.

6) She sought common ground, building alliances between women and men, rich and poor, powerful and powerless.

Elizabeth Fry, my historic heroine, became a good steward and a great neighbor. She began with economic surplus and gradually developed emotional surplus, cognitive surplus, spiritual surplus and a double surplus of willpower. She could have enjoyed the pleasures of high society like her six sisters, but chose to put her wealth to use with women prisoners who lacked basic necessities. Elizabeth Fry shared her surplus despite strong family objections and social ostracism. She was nurtured in giving as she nurtured a daily relationship with God. Through prayer she was transformed from an insecure girl with frequent maladies into a woman unified in body-soul-heart-mind-will-and-strength. As her image on banknotes continues to testify, this woman beautifully embodied all the elements named by Jesus in The Great Invitation.

Linking love and money, Mrs. Fry and other coddled women of privilege discovered that they could bring about significant social change in their hierarchical, patriarchal class-bound society. Together they sought common ground as Elizabeth Fry put it, "*by linking the higher and lower orders of society together.*" Under her leadership, countless Victorian women became activists through membership in The British Ladies Association, themselves becoming a powerful example of surplus, of '*being more than what is needed.*'

NEIGHBORING   BELONGING
DAN and BILL of CHUCKAWALLA VALLEY STATE PRISON:
FREE BEHIND BARS

*The truth will set you free but first it will scare the
daylightsout of you.*   Gregg Levoy

Is the prisoner my neighbor? Jesus thought so. It took me a long time to agree. My jaws still clench each time I enter a prison to bring Alternatives to Violence workshops to convicted felons. I must show ID,

76

sign log books, pocket an alarm pad, submit to search, pass through electronically-controlled gates and checkpoints. Alternatives to Violence workshops are always co-facilitated. On this occasion I represent the 'outside" with two men who comprise the 'inside team." Dazzling Dan has been imprisoned for twenty-one years and expects to die behind bars. Brilliant Bill is covered in tattoos, symbols of the violence that led to his life sentence. Mentoring these men is a *'life-glad"* experience for me. I chose Joyous Judith as my adjective name, delighted to know these neighbors.

HANK and RAUL: TWO LIFERS TELL IT LIKE IT IS

> *For everyone will be salted with fire.*
> Gospel of Mark 9:49

I wondered what might be about to happen when two inmates made a beeline for me during a coffee break toward the close of a three-day workshop in a remote desert prison. *"Will you do something for us?"* the two men asked in one voice. Uh-oh, I tensed. What if they want me to break the rules? Hunky Hank, the African-American, came right to the point. *"You offer AVP workshops at the Youth Facility in Chino, right? WE met there"* he said with a grin, gesturing at his Latino friend. Real Raul chimed in, *"Yeah, we got in trouble when we were kids. Hank and I were cellies there and now we're cellies here.*
    Here's what we want you to do, OK? Next time you go to the Youth Facility will you give those boys a message from two lifers? Tell them that we didn't have any AVP when we were young. Tell those guys to pay attention and then to take what they learn out onto the streets of Los Angeles. Tell them how these Alternatives to Violence games bond guys tighter than gangbanging does. Tell those boys what we know, that AVP trumps race and gang identity. Tell them that if we'd learned this stuff when we were their age, and if we'd had the sense to use it when we got out the first time, we wouldn't be in prison now for the rest of our lives."

INMATES SPEAK OUT: SALTY WORDS FROM MEN IN BLUE

Lively Lennie: *I seek truth and every person shares different truths.*

Intelligent Isaac: AVP *taught me to think before I react, no matter what the situation is. I can't change the past but the future can be good if I take time to make good decisions.*

77

Happy Jose: *I would like to share this program with people that doesn't speak English. This is a great program and Spanish speakers deserve it. It helps me not misjudge people or think bad about them if I don't know them.*

Joking Joe: *I learned to see the good that is inherent in all. I will be more patient and appreciative of others.. AVP meets a dire need for inmates.*

Ravishing Rick: *I am still a good person, no matter my situation. AVP has shown me how to solve things nonviolently and taught me ways to help younger people to stay out of trouble.*

Blessed Brandon: *Everyone was unified of heart and spirit.*

EARTHCARE   RESTORING
RASHEDA'S STORY FROM BANGLADESH: SECURING WATER

> *When we truly discover love, capitalism will not be possible*
> *and Marxism will not be necessary.*   Will O"Brien

Women who live in 'Burned Slum" a cluster of tin and bamboo shacks in Kalyanpur, cook outdoors and use open gutters as toilets. Five years ago the only source of water for the slum's 500 families came intermittently from a tap illegally connected to the city water facility. Women and children had to line up for two or three hours to collect each pitcher. Buckets of water from nearby houses required bribing guards, paying exorbitant prices or suffering beatings from caretakers. *"We had to get up very early to get water for the family,"* reports Rasheda Begum, a 25-year-old garment factory worker. *"We often incurred the wrath of husbands and in-laws when we were delayed."* The women and men of Burned Slum work in factories or construction sites, as lorry drivers, rickshaw pullers, trash pickers and domestic helpers. Like most Bangladeshis they live on less than a dollar a day and have little social power.

These facts did not stop Rasheda. She gathered the slum women to work together toward a legal *'water point'* connection. Mr. Mohammad Nurul Hudu Mian, manager of the water agency, insisted that water could only be given to legal land-title holders or house owners. The slum women held no titles but they would not give up. They went to DSK, an organization formed to promote health, clean water and sanitation. In 1998 The United Nations Development Programme had joined forces with DSK to help slum dwellers help themselves. After that the situation changed. *"The law still doesn't permit it,"* admits Mr. Mian,v *"but the rules are relaxed a bit due to social considerations."*

Today Rasheda and her neighbors wash with water from a well dug behind their shack. They drink and cook with fresh water from the slum's *'water point,'*—two hand pumps drawing from an underground reservoir. Persistence pays, women celebrate and domestic violence diminishes.

EARTHCARE   RESTORING
EVOLUTIONARY EFFERVESCENCE
                METAMORPHOSIS: IMAGINAL CELLS

What would happen if one day when we wake up, we realize that we are the majority?   Mario Benedetti

Imaginal cells are the key to the amazing grace of metamorphosis. Observe the clumsy, crawling, voracious worm called caterpillar. Watch it transform into the graceful, flying, subtle beauty called butterfly. How does such a miracle happen? Evolutionary biologists identified imaginal cells, which resonate at a different frequency, embedded in the tissue of each caterpillar. Imaginal cells are so unlike majority cells that the worm's immune system considers them enemies and tries to kill them. The more the worm eats, the more imaginal cells grow, more and more appearing until the caterpillar's immune system cannot destroy them. Imaginal cells become larger and stronger, connecting until they form critical mass and transform caterpillar into the beauty of butterfly.

"*I firmly believe, along with others,*" affirms Deepak Chopra, "*that there is an evolutionary effervescence within the tissues of established society today. In spite of the prevailing clamor of fear, greed, over-consumption and violence expressed through the tissues of society, there is a coming together of imaginal cells that are visioning a different world, a transformation, a metamorophosis.*"

Chopra, founder of The Alliance for a New Humanity, remembers the wisdom of anthropologist Margaret Mead. In 1969 she said "*Never doubt that a small group of thoughtful, committed citizens can change the world. Indeed, it's the only thing that ever has.*" With Mead and Chopra the author of this guide is convinced that imaginal cells are gathering everywhere, recognizing each other and collaborating to transform society from caterpillar to butterfly. You and I contain imaginal cells. So do your friends, families, co-workers, congregations and neighbors. Let us commit to continue clustering, connecting, collaborating and creating a more just and loving world.

CHAPTER TEN
SPIRITUAL PRACTICES: DIVING DEEP

Keeping Sabbath means trusting God to be God and recognizing that I am not indispensable.   Marjorie Thompson

A BASIC SACRED PRACTICE:
LOVING AND BEING LOVED

You are honored in my sight, and precious, and I love you.
                                                Isaiah 43:4

Freedom emerges from a spiritual source, not a human one. Spirituality may be an overused and misused term, but it does communicate what people experience. The core meaning of *spirituality* refers to *energy, to life force, to the breath of life.* Spirit is power that brings everything to life and forms human motivations. Spirituality is both profound and basic to existence. No matter how loved and free we're told we are, it's natural to feel blocked sometimes, unable to receive the blessings of the moment. When a reminder of original value would be welcome, turn to Isaiah 43:4 and meditate on God's blessed assurance: *You are honored in my sight, and precious, and I love you.*

SEED EXPERIENCE:
FROM TERROR TO PRAYER

Thank God for an unhappy childhood!
                                                Ellen Burstyn

Forgotten fears from childhood can unconsciously block our choice to meditate or pray. Past pain can block present-moment awareness. Pleasant memories can also grab attention when we try to quiet the mind. Nostalgia prefers the past. Nostalgically indulging in memories of comfort or solace dilutes natural Essence. Focusing attention on the past blocks contact with the present, leading to loss of intimacy, responsibility and ecstasy. Lost in nostalgia, you and I lose freedom.

The past has value when we go there intentionally. Some of the queries in Chapter Five and the writing prompts in this chapter direct attention toward experiences now behind us. Revisiting the past helps us learn from our errors. It frees stuck energies to move on. Humans create meaning by looking back in the light shed by the history of our species, our religious tribe or our loved ones. But escaping into reverie during meditation misses the mark and blocks Presence.

Fantasy expresses a preference for living in the future. For all its attractions and distractions, fantasy also dilutes Essence. People lose contact with the stimulus of crisis, moments of sensory intensity and the mysteries of Spirit-infused moments. Focusing on the future can be useful to renew hope, provide vision and hone direct action. But escaping into future fantasies also misses the mark, blocking access to The Really Real.

A CONTEMPLATIVE WAY TO PRACTICE PRESENCE
WITH ONE *THOUGHT-WORD*

Linking a single thought-word with the breath, and inwardly saying it over and over, is a time-honored way to direct attention toward the Holy. Repeating one word can, of course, lead the mind to generate many word-thoughts but the intention of this form of Centering Prayer is to use a single sacred word as a way into wordless presence at the Source.

PRACTICE STEPS WITH A WORD

Offer a simple prayer of desire to go through everything to its open source in God.

Choose to let whatever comes go to Love, into the heart of Christ.

Take several long, slow breaths and notice your contents of mind.

Gently let each thought, image, sound and feeling pass by.

Let a short word rise from your center, a word resonant with desire for presence.

Inwardly say *honored* if you like Isaiah's verse,

or *precious*, or *loved*.

When the right thought-word has come to you, renew your intent to effortlessly fall through that word into wordless, spacious presence.

If anything rises to ripple the still surface of your mind, gently go back to your thought-word and repeat it inwardly.

Seek nothing for a while but steady, trusting, attentive rest in the Source of Love.

Remain very still and let everything else go.

Open your self to cleansing, loving, radiant, healing holy presence.
Gently return to ordinary consciousness with songs of praise, feelings of appreciation or words such as The Lord's Prayer.

Questions for Reflection:
How did your word affect your desire to sink into stillness?
Were there moments of distrust or desire to produce an idea or possess a memory with your mind?
Did you get an inkling of Reality beyond control?

A DEFICIT PRACTICE:
POVERTY QUIZ

1- What percent of poor children are in families with at least one working parent?   a) 25% b) 45% c) 65%

2-What portion of U.S. Jobs pay too little to keep a family of four out of poverty?   a) one tenth   b) one quarter   c) one third

3- Since 1999 the number of poor families has grown faster in
        a) central cities   b) suburbs

4- Incomes below the poverty line among U.S. persons are most likely to be
a) White   b) Black   c) Hispanic   of any race   d) Asian   e) American Indian or Alaskan Native

5-Which racial/ethnic group has the highest percentage of people living in poverty?   a) White   b) Black   c) Hispanic   of any race
        d) Asian   e) American Indian or Alaskan Native

6-In 2005, 37 million people were officially considered 'poor'. About how many of these people were living in extreme poverty with incomes below half of the poverty threshold?
        a) 15 million   b) 10 million   c) 5 million

7- About what percentage of elders in the U.S. would be poor if they did not receive Social Security benefits?
        a) 10 percent   b) 25 percent   c) 50 percent

8- About what percentage of elders in the U.S. are poor, even though they do receive Social Security benefits?

    a) 10 percent   b) 25 percent   c) 50 percent

9- At the 350 largest public companies, the average CEO earned 11.6 million dollars in 2005. How long does it take the average CEO to earn the annual pay of a full-time minimum wage worker?

    a) 2 hours   b) 6 hours   c) 1 day

Answers to Poverty Quiz: 1-c, 2-b, 3-c, 4-a, 5-e, 6-a, 7-c, 8-a, 9-a
        For more information contact
        Friends National Committee on Legislation

CIRCLES OF EXPLORATION
FREE TO SHED LIGHT ON DEFICIT

"As far as we can discern, the sole purpose of human existence is to kindle a light in the darkness of mere being."

Carl Jung

GUIDELINES for WORSHIP SHARING in the MANNER OF FRIENDS

Once money matters to the extent that it moves from the secret folds of our wallets to the places where it is given, exchanged and forgiven, then any decisions we make about money are enhanced by shared wisdom.

Jean Stairs

Invite a few trusted friends or members of your congregation to do the preceding meditation together, or some variation of your own choosing. Afterward, share gently:

SPEAKING
    We speak from the heart, out of personal experience and feelings:
    We avoid generalizations beyond our direct experience.
    We speak only for ourselves, out of the silence.
    We may pass now and perhaps speak later on any query.
    We speak only once until everyone has had a chance to speak.
LISTENING
    In the silence after words, we hold in the Light what we heard.

We do not answer, disagree, dispute or comment to anyone.

We do not try to solve another person's problems.

We respect confidentiality. We repeat nothing outside the group that we heard from others within it.

While others are speaking we listen attentively rather than tuning them out to prepare what we will say.

We seek to hear what God may be saying to us through the words of another, especially when we feel resistant to them.

GOOD ORDER

We are mindful of the allotted time, so everyone can share.

If necessary the facilitator will remind us of time limitations.

We support the facilitator's efforts to maintain good order.

We trust the Spirit to guide our group.

SUGGESTED QUERIES

What would you change or add to the reflections above?

To whom are you accountable as you make changes?

How might you support one another moving toward greater financial freedom?

INVITATIONAL QUESTIONS

How does debt suck the life out of people?

Out of you?

Do any spiritual perspectives shed light on the different qualities of life experienced by debt-free people as well as by those who are debt-enslaved?

How might spiritual practices of LIGHT bridge economic gaps and mend rifts between people of privilege and people living in poverty?

STUFF: SPIRITUALITY IN ACTION
A GROWN-UP FIELD TRIP

Field trips were a grand adventure during elementary school. The purpose was educational, of course, but it was great fun to get out of the classroom and go somewhere interesting. Today your grown-up mission, should you choose to accept it, is to design and enjoy your own consumer field trip. Not with others, though. This is a solo educational experience.

In the spirit of The Buddhist Peace Fellowship we call it "Field Trip as Spiritual Practice."

To prepare for this consumer adventure, begin by identifying your favorite form of shopping. I am entranced by paper goods at Staples. Michael's inner compass is set to Fry's Electronics. Penelope picks up new shoes passing through Macy's. Ray gets mesmerized by art supplies. Sue stocks up on household needs at Costco. Dean can't resist bargain wines and foods at Trader Joe's.

> *List three of your favorite retail outlets.*
> *Which is most irresistible today?*

Your mission is to go there soon.

Approach it as an opportunity for spiritual practice, a walking meditation in a retail store.

What do you see, smell, hear, touch, taste and feel?

Stroll slowly and mindfully, registering whatever you find pleasing, annoying or tantalizing.

Jotting on a card or notebook I NOTICE THAT I...

Keep noticing and recording whatever comes to awareness—...sensations... images...emotions... sensations...questions...inspirations... Pay exquisite attention to your attractions and aversions. When this time of retail mindfulness seems complete, rest quietly and describe your experience in detail.

A CIRCLE of WARMTH
   SEARCHING INQUIRY PRACTICE WITH OTHERS

Should you wish to engage with friends or family in a retail field trip, here are guidelines for debriefing together. SEARCHING INQUIRY is a time-tested practice in many traditions including Buddhists, Quakers and Twelve-Step participants. Inquiry is most fruitfully done in small groups, asking questions and listening respectfully.

Each person speaks only once until everyone has had a turn.
Refrain from comments or questions, leaving each speaker free.
Reach deep for what is most true for you....

How can I best describe this retail environment to someone who does not share my affinity?

To a person who has never been inside this store?

What did I buy?

What did I choose not to buy?

How am I feeling now about the decisions I made?

What was the taste of craving like while I was totally surrounded by favorite stuff?

What did I discover about my own ability to balance on the delicate edge between need and desire?

Where is the beginning of my own slippery slope?

When and how do I sense myself sliding from desire to greed?

What new promptings or choices am I aware of now?

A PLAYFUL SABBATH PRACTICE
PURGE THE URGE TO SPLURGE

A Martian anthropologist might conclude that
The Mall is our American place of worship.
Vicki Robin

Shop-aholism can be every bit as addictive as work-aholism or alcoholism. While consumer moderation may be a virtue, it takes more than virtue to convert most of us from the religion of shopping. Conversion involves imagination, willpower and the willingness to seek out attractive alternatives. There is freedom in discovering and re-discovering free and low-cost activities that yield equal or greater pleasure than shopping. Alternate activities can take on a whole new meaning when enjoyed with someone you love. I leave these to your imagination.

Scan the list below—*Fifty Simple Things To Do Instead Of Shopping.*
Check those that kindle your imagination

Add your own good ideas

Mark the most interesting ones

Identify persons you'd like to do activities with

Write your Top Ten in bold colors

Post the list on your refrigerator

Ready, get set, go.

TO PURGE THE URGE TO SPLURGE, I CAN CHOOSE TO

1) Go on a picnic   2) Go for a walk   3) Phone a friend
4) Watch the clouds   5) Take a hike   6) Look at the stars
7) Read a book   8) Teach someone to read
9) Volunteer someplace   10) Learn to maintain my own car
11) Study another language   12) Learn geography
13) Study nature   14) Go to a nearby botanical garden
15) Go to the zoo   16) Go to a local museum
17) Make music   18) Join a choral group   19) Draw a picture
20) Take photos   21) Write on any topic that comes to mind
22) Write a letter to someone I know
23) Write to a stranger in prison
24) Write to my congress people
25) Write for human rights   26) Write a letter to the editor
27) Dance on the grass until you fall down   28) Join a club
29) Start a club   30) Clean a house   31) Have a garage sale
32) Write a will   33) Write a shopping list
34) Splurge economically at a thrift store
35) Splurge in service by shopping for a shut-in
36) Be a "purchasing agent" for a shelter or hospice
37) Count my money and know exactly how much I earn, spend, give, owe and own   38) Garden
39) Take flowers or vegetables to someone
40) Bake bread and share a loaf   41) Make soup and give some away
42) Invite guests over to share a meal
43) Practice "heart-sharing," beginning with silence, speaking one at a time and listening with total attention.
44) Reach out to someone in tender, non-erotic touch
45) Touch myself with kindness
46) Make love with care and respect
47) Meditate   48) Chant   49) Visualize world peace
50) Do nothing.

If you can truly do nothing, you are free.

"Women control most of the dollars in this country. If you see that something is harmful, stop buying it. I promise you, things will change."

Teresa Heinz Kerry

STUFF: SIMPLIFYING
PRACTICING WITH FIRE: THY WILL BE DONE

All of you are kindlers of fire, lighters of firebrands. Walk in
the flame of your fire and among the brands that you have
kindled.   Isaiah 50:11

The radiance of Sabbath Economics moves us from outwardly
reciting prayers to inwardly listening for soul. Accepting the great
invitation to love with all our heart and mind, soul and strength is to stop
standing back from the heat and to enter the fiery furnace of fiscal and social
change. Uniting contemplation with activism is to move from second-hand
learning to direct knowing. We no longer need to shiver in the cold or
shadow-box in the dark. Praying with fire brings another level of spiritual
and financial possibility into view.

Hot tempers and cold hearts alike are held tenderly by the Source of
Love. The Great Invitation leads toward wholeness. You and I need not be
whole before approaching Holy Power. Whenever we show up in prayer
the Fiery Mystery is near, ready to melt us, mold us, fill us and use us in
greater service to a hurting world. Bad habits are burned away in the
warmth of Sabbath prayer. More of who we are comes into view.
Transforming Fire kindles God's freeing presence within us even if full
freedom is not yet a felt reality.

Contemplative prayer lets us see ourselves as we are and the world
as it is, for we do not pray alone but securely warmed by the goodness and
mercy of Love. When self-awareness is fired by prayer, people begin to
recognize real needs, limits and failings. Human frailties may have led us
into debt but as we *"walk in the flame of our fire"* Holy Fire reveals who
we are in God's image. *"Forgive us our debts"* might also become
"Forgive us our stuff." Inner shifts open our eyes to see true needs and real
surplus. Over time, Sabbath rest and meditation may lead to contemplation,
defined by Douglas Steere as *"a continual condition of prayerful sensitivity*
to what is really going on."

PRAYING THY WILL BE DONE

The Lord's Prayer is the monarch of prayers, summation of
the Gospels, essence of faith;   to receive its gifts, one need
only approach it with open mind, clean heart and good will.
That God will respond is certain.   Philip Zaleski

World religious traditions agree in their assessment of the human condition which is visible within us and all around us. The Buddha portrays it this way: *"The mind is on fire, thoughts are on fire...and with what? With the fire of greed, the fire of resentment and the fire of infatuation."*

When we get quiet for awhile most of us recognize something amiss in the inmost ground of our soul. Despite our talk of free will, most of us know that we are enslaved by the appetites of our hearts, minds and bodies. We realize how quickly we get derailed by envy, anger and lust for sensual pleasure. You and I are too often afire with desire for praise and honor, far from being able to accept the great invitation to love self, God and neighbor. In stillness we are apt to hear eternal questions directed to ourselves:

> Where are you?
> What is the state of your will?
> Where do you stand?
> Are you on the way,
> or standing in the way?

The will of God, timeless and pervasive throughout eternity, nonetheless does not compel any one of us to conform to it. We are free to shut ourselves off from the grace of Love. The Creator eternally seeks our willingness. God's will is as near as our breath, ready to be a guiding authority, a healing influence, and a soothing balm to body and soul.

PRACTICE STEPS with FIRE
OPENING MY WILL TO THY WILL

For five minutes, with eyes closed, count by number everything that registers in your mind—thoughts, sensations, sounds, concepts, feelings, desires, self-images.
Do not try for anything, just let your mind be it's usual way.

Instead of attaching to or avoiding thoughts, simply count them.

For another five minutes see if you can notice the spaces between thoughts.
Choose to linger in the zone behind and between ideas, desires & emotions.
Whenever something comes into awareness, gently let it pass by.

For the final ten minutes or so, notice what comes up but instead of counting, try to see each image or idea as a bubble of divine will rising to consciousness.

Open yourself like a question-mark to the holy liberating presence.

Listen for anything shaped for you that seems to come from God.

Questions for Reflection:

What relationship did you notice between your own will, background spaciousness of thoughts, and a *'felt sense'* of the Sacred?

What happened for you in the spaces behind and between thoughts?

What was it like for you to mute *"my will"* and invite *"thy will"* during this contemplative practice?

"The prayer Jesus gave us," concludes *The Prayer of Fire* author Lorraine Kisly, *"is complete, peerless and indestructible....May an ever-deepening encounter with The Lord's Prayer accomplish in us what Christ intends."*

LIVING BREAD FOR SPIRITUAL HUNGER:
TASTING WITH FULL AWARENESS

Take. Eat. Do this in remembrance of me.   Jesus

PRACTICE STEPS WITH BREAD

Wine-tasters enjoy the art of comparative appreciation. In the spirit of wine tasting, invite some favorite folks to join you for a fine bread-tasting.

Select three different varieties of bread and arrange pieces on three plates. Smell the first bread, inhaling the fragrance for a full minute. Describe the scent in memories—

"This reminds me of a summer picnic with Aunt Sadie"
or in metaphors—*"this bread is like a Walt Whitman poem."*

Explore each aroma and describe each variety.

Take your time, playfully enjoying each bread.

Take a bite of bread into your mouth and hold it lightly for a little while.

Swirl it around on your tongue, chewing tenderly.

Savor the taste and texture before you swallow the bread.
What colors dance on your tongue?
Which physical sensations show on your face?
What tune of flavor do you sing or hum?

Questions for Reflection:
How do you describe your food choices to others? To your self?
How do you define healthy food? Comfort food?
What is your mood after a quick meal?
A slow meal?

SABBATH ECONOMICS: LIVING WATER FOR A THIRSTY AGE
GAZING INTO TRANSPARENCY

When I look into water it feels like I'm seeing the world on the seventh day, when everything is new and just itself—before the snake, and the tears, and the explanations.

Joan Acocelk

PRACTICE STEPS WITH WATER

Indoors, fill a clear bowl or pitcher with water and sit close.
Outdoors, sit near a pool or stream, lake or sea.
Close your eyes and offer a prayer of intention to be fully present.
Open eyes, reaching with your will toward the sacred.

Let yourself become hollowed out, receptive, as transparent as you can be.
Open yourself to the One who loves you through and through.
There is nothing to think about, just pure clear being.
Gaze into the water in stillness for twenty minutes or so.

Questions for Reflection:
What was it like to let yourself become transparent?
How much trust and openness did you sense?
How much anxiety or boredom?
Was there a graced moment of any kind?

NEIGHBORS: BELONGING
  SALT AS TRANSFORMATIVE ELEMENT
  STANDING ROCK-SOLID

You will know the truth and the truth will make you free.
  Gospel of John 8:32

What does the word 'truth' mean? Is it just religious rhetoric? Religions do have oppressive aspects but freedom is the core spiritual teaching in most faith traditions. Because we, the people, are fairly self-centered, it is easy to become at odds with ourselves. While not necessarily "selfish" the average perspective is limited by being self-preoccupied. Self-centeredness leads to thinking that liberty means doing what we want to do when we want to do it. The problem is that what we think we want seldom reflects our true needs or our true nature. In fact, self-centered wants often tend to conflict with real needs. Humans can be, and often are, slaves to our own fears, feelings, appetites and aversions. This is why most of us seem to need divine assistance

PRACTICE STEPS: SLOW WALKING:
  A SACRED PRACTICE TO DO ANYTIME, ANYPLACE

Stand in a circle if in a group, at least arm's length apart. If alone make sure you have enough space to walk in a circle or straight line without encumbrance.
  Take several long slow breaths while seeking holy ground.
    Turn to your left so that you will be moving clockwise.
      Lift your left foot about six inches off the ground.
        Extremely slowly, bring it forward just half a step so your left heel comes down at your right instep.

Keep eyes unfocused, on the ground several feet ahead of you.
  Lift your right foot very slowly and evenly and put it down half a step ahead.
    Let feet, breath and mind continually flow together, in this moment.
      Lifting feet just an inch or two helps keep your balance.

Sense the spaciousness of the present moment.
  Continue for 20 minutes, longer if you can.

Questions for Reflection:
> Did you notice moments of unself-conscious movement in the flow?
>> Did your mind ever fall behind or leap ahead of your feet?
>>> What does all this suggest about how you stand and move?
>>>> What was different about slow-walking by yourself and with others?

NEIGHBORING: BELONGING
>SALT AS TRANSFORMATIVE ELEMENT
>>SAVORING THE PSALTER

> *This is not a method but rather a type of free-form serious play.* Kathleen Norris

PRACTICE STEPS WITH LECTIO DIVINA

Lectio divina is an ancient practice of meditating on scripture. In this spiritual form of reading, the reader seeks to enhance and deepen awareness rather than knowledge. Whether you choose bible passages, poetry or personal love letters, enjoy reading the words aloud, trying out different voices. You may wish to memorize a verse or two and let it move through consciousness while going about daily life.

Read Nan Merrill's version of Psalm 32: 1-7 below.

> Read it aloud three times, slowly, if you like.
>> Pray a Psalm solo, or with other people.
>>> Listen for a word or phrase that 'shimmers' for you.

> Carry it silently on your breath for ten or twenty minutes.
>> Notice what comes to your attention, then let it go.
>>> Breathing in and breathing out, return to stillness.
>>>> Drop through the word into Holy Presence.

Blessed is each one whose wrongdoings have been forgiven,
> *whose shame has been forgotten.*
Blessed is each one in whom Love Divine finds a home,

and whose spirit radiates truth.

When I acknowledged not my shortcomings,
*   I became ill through all my defenses.*
Day and night, guilt weighed heavy in my heart;
*   my spirit became dry as desert bones.*

I admitted my faults to the Most High, and I made known my regret;
*   I cried out "Forgive me, O Comforter, for those times*
*   I have sinned in my thoughts, my words and my deeds."*

And the Beloved created a clean heart within me.

Therefore, let anyone who is sincere give thanks to the Beloved;
*   For whenever we feel overwhelmed by fear,*
*   We shall be embraced by Love.*
Dwelling in the heart of the Beloved, we are free from distress,
*   Free to live creatively.*

A SABBATH CIRCLE OF TRUST
FREE TO HEAR AFRESH

While reading scripture you may hear a "hum: in your inner
ear, a HUM of intimate encounter that connects reader, text
and divine voice.   Avivah Zornberg

Gather some interested people in a comfortable place.   Review
WORSHIP SHARING GUIDELINES and print copies for each participant
if you wish.

After a few minutes of quiet, take turns reflecting aloud, responding only to
the following queries that hum for you …

Which translation of the Bible appeals to me the most?
    Which translation of scripture do I like the least?
        Which parts of the Bible do not hum for me?

Imagine God with a tuning fork, attuning some selected lines of poetry,
fiction or Psalms directly to your soul.
    Which words or quotes resonated for me when I was young?
        Do I still remember anything once committed to memory?

What words now stir my heart and soul?
Tickle   my mind?
Strengthen my will?

Do any of these ancient words offer a new bowl for my soul?
Did a salty image beckon me nearer to truth and freedom?
Where might Love be leading me?

EARTHCARE: RESTORING
AIR AS TRANSFORMATIVE ELEMENT
BREATHING FREELY

Everyone needs beauty as well as bread, places to play in and pray in where Nature may heal and cheer and give strength to body and soul alike.   John Muir

So much is freely given.   Creation freely offers life-sustaining elements of air, water, light and fire.   Earth provides life-preserving elements of salt, seed and soil.   We, the people, can breathe, rest, eat and play. We can hear music, see beauty, smell bread and taste salt.   Could it be that praying is a sense as natural to humans as hearing, sight, smell and taste? When Essence gets damaged, the ability to pray may get lost and we require assistance to reclaim innate capacities.

A SACRED PRACTICE TO DO ANYTIME, ANYPLACE:
BREATHING OPEN

Breath symbolizes life throughout The Bible from Genesis—*God breathed life into Adam* (2:7)—to Revelation—*a breath of life from God entered them (11:11)*. More specifically, breath is the symbol of Ultimate Life (*ruach* in Hebrew, *pneuma* in Greek) inspiriting human life. Focusing on our breath is the simplest way of releasing bodily tension and slowing busy minds. Deep sighs and yawns are instinctive ways of calling our attention to breathing. This exercise is one way of opening to the Sacred by slowing the breath.

PRACTICE STEPS with AIR

Lightly notice the speediness of your breath and thoughts.

95

Remember your desire for Love through a wordless feeling or image.

     Begin breathing deep down into your diaphragm-stomach.

     Put your hands there and feel it swell out and in.

Gradually fill your lungs from this deep point upward.

     Release your breath very slowly, twice as slowly as you breath in.

     Pause briefly at the bottom of your breath cycle with a still mind.

     Pause in stillness again at the point of fullness.

Continue with the specific intent of breathing in all that is of Love and breathing out all that is not.

     You need not think of anything else.

     If attention wanders simply refresh your intent to be fully filled from with all that is of Love and to empty yourself of whatever is not.

     Rest in a spacious place, confidently grounded in Presence.

Questions for Reflection:

     Did slow breathing seem to make any difference to your sense of presence?

     Can you think of ways that your breathing habits lead to distraction?

     When and where might you practice open breathing daily?

CHAPTER ELEVEN
GO FOR THE GOLD: MINING YOUR EXPERIENCE

GOING FOR THE GOLD

Much is wrong in the world. Valid criticism can be directed toward the harm done by large and small economic forces but this guide chooses to focus on people who bring creative energy to economic, ecological and relational problems. No ink will be spent on what is wrong but will highlight folks who align money matters with spiritual values and vision. This guide wants to focus on the gold.

The first wave of Gold Rush miners panned by hand and found the largest nuggets. When those had been taken, hydraulic mining operators began pumping river water through narrow brass nozzles. Imagine a hardy crew, the second wave of Gold Rushers working in the Feather River— filling hoses, directing forceful streams of water through narrow nozzles, washing away layers of sediment and finally getting to buried gold. You are invited to aim attention and intention toward what lies beneath social conventions. Economic woes are the topic of many *'ain't it awful'* conversations but such talk doesn't change anything. The gold of economic freedom is still buried under stony habits and attitudes.

Combining the wisdom of The Great Invitation with the household practices of Sabbath Economics gives our generation of miners another way to go for the gold.

How does personal self-examination and theological reflection help?

Directed inquiry uncovers gold of meaning and purpose hidden beneath habitual ways you and I manage love and money. Such labors reveal more options, greater joy and more generous giving and serving, the direction and goal of Sabbath Economics. It is work, yes, but less sweaty than holding high-pressure hoses to wear away rock. Instead we use stories, spiritual practices and endless queries to move tons of worthless gravel out of the way.

SABBATH PRESENCE THEN—WRITING A LOVE POEM

Growing up, I remember a place my young self felt safe, free and happy...
I recall the sensory pleasures of childhood, recording some that I loved...
Sounds I loved to hear....

Sights I loved to see ...

Smells I loved to sniff ...

Foods I loved to taste ...

Items I loved to touch ....

People I loved to be with ....

Places I loved to play ....

Places I loved to pray ....

Something God loves about me is ....

SABBATH PRESENCE NOW
HOW DO I PERCEIVE THE HOLY ONE?

> *Who do you say that I am?*   Luke 9:20

Private perceptions of divine identity matter. Personal images
matter a lot. If I perceive God as Commander-in-Chief then I am bound to
follow orders no matter how much harm is done. If I perceive God as high-
and-mighty Lord, then I have no access to "his" throne unless armed guards
permit me to enter the castle. If I perceive God as stern and distant Judge, I
would have to be pretty desperate before daring to approach "his" bench.

How do I perceive the Creator in seasons of economic security?
When I am struggling through times of financial chaos?
When I am celebrating the joy of new love?
When I am grieving the loss of a loved
one?

St. Augustine mined his memories. In his *Confessions* Augustine reported
a moment when he experienced Holy Presence *"with a click of the heart."*

You might wonder…

> How do I experience God's presence or lack of it these days?
> Have I ever had a sudden "click" of divine awareness?
> Who was the Holy One for me at that moment?

GETTING STARTED
WRITING YOUR MONEY AUTOBIOGRAPHY

> *I'd like to hand this manuscript to you—*
> *Wherever you are,*
> *Whoever you are—and say*
> *'This is how it is with me: how is it with you?*
> Nelle Morton

- A favorite implement to write with then….now
- Your memory of the first book you read about love
- When did you keep a diary or journal?   What happened?
- A moment when you were silent but wanted to speak
- A poem you love
- A favorite woman writer
- A hero who fights injustice and oppression
- A heroine who befriends the poor
- A group you admire who works to restore nature
- A favorite word—use it in a sentence
- A demonstration you have attended
- Your thoughts on that
- A favorite spiritual writer
- An adult who saw your potential when you were young
- A time when God grabbed your attention
- A way you pray when you hear sirens
- A time when play or laughter has brought you closer to God
- A way you exercise your imagination
- A person in the Bible you identify with
- A time of belonging in a group or congregation
- One person or idea that has expanded your idea of prayer
- One idea you have about bringing Sabbath into daily life

DEFICIT: OWING
　　　LIGHT AS TRANSFORMATIVE ELEMENT
　　　　　LIVING DAYLIGHT

Your money or your life!" We know what to do when a burglar makes this demand, but not what to do when God does.　　　　　　　　Mignon McLaughlin

"It scared the living daylights out of me!" she wailed.

'I'll beat the living daylights out of you," he threatened.

Threats linking fear with light terrified me in childhood. Long-forgotten times of being made to feel *"not-okay"* constrained my young soul, and possibly yours, too. Doubts and fears conveyed by caregivers may have catapulted some of us into adulthood with a sense of *"not-enoughness,"* a vague sense of insufficiency. Uneasiness about emptiness is familiar to most people, emptiness rooted in loss of Essence when we were very young. The personal sense of deficit is not a truly empty state, though. Whenever we tumble into an unconscious zone of *not-okay not-enoughness* our hearts tend to fill with distressing feelings, our minds fill with confusing thoughts and our bodies flood with uncomfortable sensations.

Living Daylight is the exact opposite of fear and doubt. Sun represents the basic goodness of existence, the natural essence of creation. It offers light and warmth, a daily benediction of love. We may experience Light along the spectrum from ordinary and simple to ecstatic and blissful, depending on what is going on within us. Living Daylight is pure goodness, grace bathing the universe. It cannot be captured, controlled or used to punish. Living Daylight is the highest form of Love, the boundless presence. And while Light is a universal religious metaphor for God, science also verifies that it is more than a metaphor. Living Daylight has power to create and transform. Eyewitness reports say that Jesus, Buddha, Mohammed were all infused with Light, an essential element of spiritual transformation that is available to all.

REFLECTING ON DEFICIT
WHAT DID I DO WHEN I HAD LESS THAN ENOUGH?

And the light shone in darkness and
Against the Word the unstilled world still whirled
About the center of the silent Word.

T.S. Eliot

Stretch your memory back, recalling a time when you did not have enough to cover your expenses. Write spontaneously for 3 minutes:

A time when I had to make a difficult money decision was ...

On a new page, draw a line down the center. Put GOOD FORTUNE at the top of one side and BAD FORTUNE on the other. Jot down brief phrases, noting times of abundance in one column and periods of adversity in the other.

Write quickly as memories come to you. Don't try to fit them into any particular order. Recall times when you felt flush and had plenty. Remember times when you felt pinched and wished you had more money. Jot down a few descriptive words in each column.

GOOD FORTUNE   *BAD FORTUNE*

When your list seems finished, check in with yourself, writing

I'm noticing that I ...

If someone trustworthy is nearby, you might want to tell each other about one experience from each column. Notice whether you want to begin with the good news or the bad news, and start there.

Take three or four minutes to describe an economic challenge that may have seemed like a curse, or a time of good fortune that seemed like a blessing. Give equal attention to times of adversity and abundance, want and plenty.

When each person's speaking seems complete, sit together in silence for a little while. Notice any ideas, feelings, promptings or physical sensations that may be moving within you. Complete your time together by sharing...   *I'm noticing that I ...I'm wondering if ...*

101

VISION AND HOPE:
   SEEING THE LIGHT

> *God may have said "Let there be light"*
> *but there was no one there to hear it.*
> *Creation was a silent act.*
>
> George R. Merrill

Vision and hope are spiritual beacons that light our darkness, revealing the lie in the cultural lure of buying happiness. Hope and vision illuminate the way our world needs to be and can become as more of us choose to exercise more conscious choices with money and love.

Rev. Dr. Martin Luther King, Jr. was led by vision and hope. Although the writer of this guide has not been to the mountaintop with Dr. King or seen the promised land that he proclaimed, I have some experience of enough-ness. It is good to be nearly free of consumer bondage and totally free of fiscal debt, with a lot of help from my friends. Consumer freedom is good, very good. Others in my Pilgrim and Quaker faith communities have thrown off retail chains, choosing to walk the path of simplicity together. No, I have not been to the mountaintop, but I have been to the mall. Out beyond the blare and glare of the great American shopping center I see green pastures and still waters. Out beyond the mall is an open field, a place of goodness and mercy. I'll meet you there.

EXPLORING DEBT: BRINGING FACTS TO LIGHT
   WHERE AM I NOW FINANCIALLY?

> *Light is a metaphor for the divine.*   Rex Ambler

PERSONALLY:
   When and how have I sought help during a money crisis?
      What strengths grew from my indebtedness?
         What would I do differently in the future?
            Where was God in all this?
   How can I learn about practical applications of simplicity?

RELATIONALLY:
   How have I helped someone during a financial emergency?

What graces emerged from this time of support?
What complications arose with family or friends?
What would I do differently next time?
Where did Love emerge?

COMMUNALLY:

How does my congregation communicate its willingness to be supportive with people who need financial help?

How do we demonstrate respect and confidentiality?

What structures does my congregation have in place to respond to urgent economic emergencies such as Becky's?

How might we become better prepared?

Do we learn together about preventable debt?

About the spiritual roots of simplicity?

STUFF   SIMPLIFYING
FIRE AS TRANSFORMATIVE ELEMENT
BEYOND CONSUMER DESIRE

It is the nature of desire not to be satisfied, and most human beings live only for the gratification of desire.   Aristotle

Some assert that the desire to acquire stuff may be rooted in a sense of inferiority. I certainly grew up with an inferiority complex; perhaps you did, too. No matter how talented, resourceful or clever I may be, someone else is always older, stronger, smarter or sweeter. For me, emotional vulnerabilities peaked in adolescence and diminished as I have, but hidden feelings of inadequacy still lurk in the corners of what Anne Lamott dubbed *"my crooked little heart."* Any sense of inadequacy is enslaving at any age. You and I want to be able to express our gifts, but feelings of unworthiness make it hard to feel confident about developing our innate capacities. Attachment to gratification can become an inner tyrant that binds us to consumer habits. *"From a spiritual perspective,"* says Gerald May, *"attachment is the complex dynamic that binds our capacity for love and altruism to self-centered desires. The root of the word, a-tache, means "nailed to."*

FIRE AS A METAPHOR FOR TRANSFORMATION

> *"Fire, which is hot by nature, makes wood hot by setting it*
> *on fire. In the same way, the whole world is lit with the fire*
> *of Being itself, which people call God. Every creature exists*
> *through participation in that fire, the mystery of divine*
> *being."*   Elizabeth Ann Johnson

I like the image of fire and the energy it releases, while also cringing with memories of being burned. Primordial fire offers a mixed metaphor for personal economic transformation. As we can attest, fire releases great energy that is potentially destructive as well as creative. Some would use the fire analogy for God. Theologian Elizabeth Ann Johnson gives it a positive spin, relating the relational nature of God to the relational dynamism of fire. *"The free overflowing of the fire of being shares this gift with creatures, setting up a relationship of participation. All creatures participate to some degree in "being," the very dynamism of existing, which God in essence is."*

Playing with fire as a personal analogy, how have you been burned?
> Paying high interest on credit card debt?
> > Getting suckered into a get-rich-quick Ponzi scheme?
> > > Do you bear scars from economic failures beyond your own, such as stock-market collapses, bank failure or bad mortgage?

Praying with fire as a transformative metaphor, how can you glean clues about the origin and value of the stuff you own?
> How do you enlist the primordial power of divine fire to burn away excess?
> > What might the flame of God's love in your life feel like?

FIERY VIEWS AND VALUES
EXPLORING CONFIDENCE AND DOUBT

> *When you walk through the fire you shall not be burned, and*
> *the flame shall not consume you.*
>
> Isaiah 43:2

My level of confidence in myself as a wise consumer, on a scale of 1 to 10
is... because ....
   I rank my level of confidence in myself as a smart investor at ...
   because
      I learn more from my successes (or failures) due to ...

Childhood ads that grabbed my attention were   (best) and (worst) ...
   Today, imagining myself as a creative advertising exec intending to
   influence children's spending , I'd use the strategy of ... to ....
      Free-write for ten minutes beginning with the phrase
         The role of advertising in forming my values and
         self-image was...

People who have contributed to my changing relationship with money are
   Social factors/religious influences that have guided my perceptions
   include...
      These days I worry about money when...
         These days money gives me pleasure and ease
         through...

STUFF   SIMPLIFYING
         PRAYING WITH FIRE

   *Some day, after mastering the winds, the waves, the tides
   and gravity, we shall harness the energies of love....Then,
   for the second time in the history of the world, humanity will
   have discovered fire.*   Pierre Teilhard de Chardin

You, dear reader, the one comfortably stretched out on the couch or
snuggled under the comforter, perhaps you are asking yourself:

Could I do any of this stuff I'm been reading about?
   Am I fiery enough to dramatically simplify my life?
      Do I even want to?
         What would happen to my identity?
            How can I let go of all the good stuff I own,
            those cool things that define who I am?

Read on if you are held captive by shopping and mesmerized by the cultural
siren song of '*bigger, newer, better, more*'. See how other folks deal with
the same dilemmas. Reflect on your own inner flame and perhaps you, too,

will "*discover energies of love*" potent enough to re-kindle your true heart's desire.

SEEING ANEW WHAT LOVE CAN DO:
FROM SURPLUS TO SIMPLICITY

"No, love is not blind, as they say ...The loving gaze does not idealize. On the contrary, love tears the covering off pseudo-reality and projects into daily life what it sees in its moments of illumination.   Anna-Natalia Malachowskaja

Consumerism and materialism stand ready to hijack our attention and resources.   Eyes blinded by cultural expectations cannot see how consumption seduces.   You and I can become shopping slaves and not even notice that we are in economic bondage.   The focused eye of the Sacred sees consumer tension among people of all tax brackets.   Sabbath Economics takes Jesus' invitation seriously, assisting people to be happy and free without "going shopping."

Human eyesight varies.   Some people are naturally near-sighted and others are far-sighted.   Dual vision is both a useful concept and my actual condition.   I don't know about you but my eyes changed as I grew older. When I balked at wearing bi-focal glasses, a wise optometrist suggested contact lenses of two different focal lengths.   The idea seemed odd but brain and eye muscles quickly learned to work together.   My corrected left eye is now far-sighted and my right eye is near-sighted.   Lenses of two different powers provide both an effective solution to aging eyes and an elegant metaphor of dual vision.

Near-sighted people see best at close range.   Gazing with the right eye shows where I am on the spectrum from consumer-driven shopping habits to freely chosen spending patterns.   Gazing with the far-sighted left eye shows where I'll end up if I keep accumulating stuff and debt.   I can see what a simple lifestyle looks like, and who else is heading for financial freedom with me on the Sabbath Economics road.   The Great Invitation is both near and far-sighted, illuminating Jesus' dual vision of a transcendently loving God who becomes immanent when we see and respond to neighbors in need. Dual beams of vision and hope reveal the lie of consumption-based 'happiness," showing the way our world needs to be, and can become, as more of us choose differently.

Sabbath Economics is both a religious idea and a spiritual practice. We recall that the root word for "*religion*" means '*to tie*" or '*to link*." Sabbath household practices link soul with money matters.   Personal lifestyle issues—deficit, giving and investing—are rooted in Sabbath, grounded in love and tied to the faith issues of simplifying, neighboring and caring for creation. Together these seven elements have plenty of fiery power, enough to transform the material and spiritual conditions of our individual and common lives.

WATER AS TRANSFORMATIONAL ELEMENT
KNOW YOUR FLOW

When you pass through the waters, I will be with you, and through the rivers, they shall not overwhelm you .Isaiah 43:2

Money relationships can easily become complicated and confusing. The complexities of economics go beyond how much or how little cash we may have. Many of us carry financial baggage—attitudes and habits—that keep us stuck. Unexamined mind-sets dam the natural flow of money through our lives until we can uncover buried truths. Stories, reflections, queries, Sabbath disciplines and practical exercises offer ways to plumb the depths and point the way toward developing our own versions of a Sabbath Economics Household Covenant. The process is simple, but not easy. Knowing your flow is nothing like drifting down the river on a summer afternoon: Probing self-examination means investing the whole self—heart, soul, mind and will—in bringing hidden money-motives into conscious view. Those who endure the journey will find it worth the effort, tapping into a wellspring of clarity, sufficiency, freedom and joy with money.

PROMPTS AND SUGGESTIONS
FORMATIVE INFLUENCES AND RELATIONSHIPS

At dinner time when I was young, our house smelled of ...
In the winter, our home was heated by ... and the air was ...
Outdoors in spring, the scent I most enjoyed...
Summer time fragrances included...
In the autumn I liked the smell of ...

When I was six the family was supported by....doing the work of ...
Assumptions my family held about money included ...
What my parents told me about buying and spending ...

Our economic status affected my sense of self, neighbor, world and God by...
The biggest financial mistake my folks ever made involved ...

107

In my family, money caused conflict and confusion when

Ten commandments that best summarize my family's values with money are...
    In childhood my relationship with money was like...
        I now deal with money just like mom, dad, aunt, grandparent or...

My current approach to money is just the opposite of (dad etc) because...
    I'm more likely to make errors of omission, or commission such as...
        The biggest money mistake I ever made...
            What I learned from it ...
                Mistakes I seem to keep repeating include
                Contributions to my pattern seem to involve...

A DROP OF DAVID JAMES DUNCAN'S TALE
    MY STORY AS TOLD BY WATER, page 11

> *...Like the water*
> *of a deep stream, love is always too much. We*
> *did not make it. Though we drink till we burst*
> *we cannot have it all, or want it all.*
> *In its abundance it survives our thirst.*
>
> Wendell Berry

"Kids tend to befriend creeks the way adults befriend each other; start shallow, and slowly work your way deeper...Then I came to water too deep to wade, too deep to see bottom: a shady black pool, surface-foam eddying like stars in a nebula. And though I wanted to keep exploring, though I'd barely begun, the big pool proved a psychic magnet...
Its surface was a night sky in broad daylight...
Its depths were another world within this one...
The entire frenetic creek stopped here to rest...
I was 78 per cent water myself ...

I felt physically ordered to crawl out on a cantilevered log, settle belly-down, and watch the pool gyre directly beneath me, the foam-starred surgace eddying, eddying, till it became a vision of night; water-skipper meteors, sun-glint novas. The creek would not stop singing. I spun and spiraled, grew foam-dazed and gyre-headed. Pieces of the mental

equipment I'd been taught to think I needed began falling into the pool and dissolving:
> *my preference of light to darkness,*
> > *sense of rightsideup and upsidedownness,*
> > > *sense of surfacees and edges,*
> > > > *sense of where I end and other*
> > > > *things or elements begin.*

The pool taught nothing but mystery and depth. An increasingly dissolved "I" followed the first verb, gravity, down. Yet depth, as the dissolved "I" sees it, is also height."

In an impassioned and often hilarious collection of essays, Duncan stirs contemplative, activist and rhapsodic views into a distinctive brew, writing with power and urgency about the vital connections between our water-filled bodies and this water-covered planet. See Resources for details on the book that Library Journal describes as *"refreshing as a glass of water on a scorching day."*

David James Duncan begins his autobiographical musings with a poem by Wendell Berry.
Which poetic voice would set the tone for your own "story of love and money as told by water"?

Duncan's chapter on Strategic Withdrawal (a naturalist's name for Sabbath time) ends on page 224 with *"this prayer: When I'm lost God help me get more lost. Help me lose me so completely that nothing remains but the primordial peace and originality that keep creating and sustaining this blood-, tear- and love-worthy world that's never lost for an instant save by an insufficiently lost me."*

SURPLUS: STEWARDING, INVESTING, GIVING

The growing gap between *"haves"* and people who *"have not"* impacts me by...
> A word, phrase or image that best represents my feeling about this...
> > Something missing in my current approach to finances is ...

For my relationship with love and money to become more free, I want to...
> The worst advice I ever received about finances was ...
> > The last time I changed my opinion on this was ...

Have I ever been deceived by my own opinions on money matters?
How do I acknowledge my mistakes and to whom?
When did I make the most of my errors?
What did that feel like?

What sources do I rely upon for charitable-giving guidance?
Who's the happiest donor I know?
Where does she/he go for counsel?
Who is the most joyful investor I know?
When might I arrange a conversation?

List three ideas I hold about investing...
How did I come to form each of them?
How firmly do I believe in each of them?
Which idea has the strongest emotional hold on me?
What might lead me to question this belief?
What might prompt me to change it?

What sources do I use to obtain and verify financial information?
Have I ever failed to heed my own experience?
How might I have been the prime cause of a bad decision?

Which people primarily influence my views on investing and donating?
Where do most of my ideas about surplus come from ...
books, TV, internet, newspapers, magazines?

How might my views and values change if I lived in a different country?
Belonged to a different faith tradition?
Ethnic group?   Economic class?
How might my ideas be different if I were 20 years older or younger?
Saw life as if I were the opposite gender?

SPIRITUAL REFLECTIONS   SALTY FREEDOM
    FREE TO TRANSFORM

Be transformed by the renewing of your mind.
Romans 12:2

Salty freedom requires skill, honesty, and practice. Just as we can learn to read scripture mindfully and heart-fully, so we can learn to read our own hearts and minds honestly.   With time and practice we can also respectfully and caringly learn to read the faces, voices and meanings of others.

The human mind is a marvelous gift, a vital cog in the wheel of freedom with love and money. The brain's task is complex, for we must learn to think through what sounds real and true, and to sort that out from what may be illusory or imagined. Cognitive capacities are essential for threshing the wheat of enduring value from the chaff of popular culture. Unused or underused, the human mental apparatus gets dusty or rusty, leaving us easily captivated by insignificant things. People need hardy stimuli to shake up dull, unthinking habits of mind, to learn to discern fact from fiction and to practice tracing out the consequences of our actions. Imaginative exercises, lively games and experiential decision-making processes foster capacities to distinguish between truth and error, illusion and reality, sense and nonsense

NEIGHBORS: BELONGING   SAVORING THE SALT

It is a covenant of salt forever before the Lord for you and your descendants as well.   Numbers 19:19

Having come this far in A SPIRITUAL GUIDE TO SABBATH ECONOMICS: MAKING LOVE WITH MONEY you may be sticking with it because of a desire for more meaning and a greater sense of purpose. Perhaps you recognize some inner blocks and barriers to freedom and fulfillment.

- Do I long to find out who I really am in relationship with God and neighbor?
- Do I wonder what kind of covenant my ancestors might have made?
- Do I ponder what holy agreements are part of my spiritual inheritance.
- Do I ask what went on ages ago that affects my loved ones in this age?
- What goes on in the heart of God without our knowledge?
- Could my ancestors have made a covenant of salt with God?
- Could commitments they made ages ago be seasoning my own life now?
- Where did this yearning come from, anyway?
- What's the source of my desire to grow closer to Love?
- What gets in the way of my best intentions?
- What blocks my ability to manage money more wisely?
- What keeps me from loving my neighbors?

EARTHCARE   RESTORING
        AIR AS TRANSFORMATIVE ELEMENT
        BREATHE THE AIR

                    I pray by breathing.

                                        Thomas Merton

    It's good that the good monk Merton didn't live at my house.
Cigarette smoke clouded the air when I was growing up. Breathing was
dangerous in home and car. Second-hand smoke damaged my lungs. Bouts
of bronchitis marked my early life but adults did not make the connection
between my childhood pneumonia and Dad's unfiltered Camels. I certainly
connected breath with survival when my brothers played rough, holding me
down and pressing pillows over my face. Pure air became more precious
than diamonds, leading me to wonder...

Could prayer be like breath, a natural human capacity?
        Are people formed with an innate breath-link to the sacred?
                What's the relationship between air and restoration?
                        What does breath have to do with cherishing our
                        earth?

UNEXPECTED GIFTS:
MARY LU COUGHLIN'S LOVE-MONEY STORY

    *When asked to write my experience with money, I hesitate because
my story is out of the ordinary. In thinking about what I want to say, I will
try to just tell my truth as simply as possible.*

    *Bottom line, everyone has their own soul's story to tell about their
experience of living with the resources that are theirs. In using the word
resources, I understand that word in a holistic sense. Resources of body,
mind, emotion, spirit.*

    *My efforts at working with my particular resources were given a
boost when I read a book in the early 80's that shared these three wisdoms
about how to approach life in a way that brought personal satisfaction.*

        No comparison.

        No judgment.

        No need to understand.

    *So to begin, my personal journey with the meaning of money and
goods started in religion class in the first grade when I was five. There
were two simple catechism questions and answers.*

Who made me?
God made me.
Why did God make me?
God made me to know, love and serve God, and
to be happy with God forever.

I remember distinctly having this inmost "ah-ha," knowing that I understood my life's purpose. As a footnote, I went on to earn the Excellence in Religion medal for my first year in school. I believe it was the only academic award of my formal educational experience.

Looking back, I have come to understand that my response to these two questions throughout my life grew out of the graces that are uniquely mine. And that in being asked to write about money, it is not about money per se but rather about how one prioritizes fulfilling the meaning of one's life.

For me, I could never get serious about making more money than I needed to meet expenses. I always worked at what was meaningful to me based on my understanding of the gospel and the words attributed to Jesusabout the poor, the beatitudes and so on. And added to my personal choices, because of family up-bringing, no matter how much I earned, some small part always went into savings for the rainy day.

Three years ago I suffered the shocking, sudden death of my brother and friend. When things settled a bit, I realized that I was the sole inheritor of his trust. This meant that my financial life took a 180-degree turn. At age 63, I had never needed an accountant, a lawyer, a financial advisor. In fact, in the prior ten years I did not earn enough to merit having to pay personal income taxes. I even needed to take early Social Security payment ($550 a month) to help pay my health insurance premiums.

What all has occurred in these three years is beyond a short summary. But the primary thought that I can share with you, dear reader, is that my lifelong relationship to money has not changed. The fundamental understanding of my purpose in life remains the same.

For the last 22 years I have joined with others in working to co-create a not-for-profit holistic healing center. It has been primarily a labor of love where we continually emphasize the quality of services and trust that the Universe will provide us with what we need.

With a resource book from Judith, I am now researching inspired philanthropy models and wanting to sit with others and dream how we can invest in programs and processes that help human beings bring their deepest needs to fulfillment and peace.

From the beginning, I have been blessed to have the inward feeling that I have and will always have what is needed. Thus, my work is to keep my eye on the prize.

CHAPTER TWELVE
LOVES OF MY LIFE—THANKS AND BLESSINGS

PEARLS BEYOND PRICE

Pete Nelson, Mary Lu Couglin, Dale Stitt, Esther Elizabeth, Anne Muree, Rick Moore, Sandee Yarlott, Ron Stief, Jim and Jan O'Donnell, Julie Steinbach, Bill Moremen, Barbara Troxell.

GENEROUS GUIDES

Ched Myers, Peg Rosenkrands, Matt Colwell, John D. Parker, Andy Loving and Susan Taylor, Lee Van Ham, Don McClanen, Vicki Curtiss, Rosemary Williams, Tracy Gary, Frank and Ruth Butler, Andy Loving, Darin Gibson, Alice Matano, Elaine Enns, Rick Zemlin, Nancy and Chuck Cooney, Joe Dominguez and Vicki Robin, Evy McDowell, Rick Kidd, Ross and Gloria Kinssler, Christopher Mogil and Anne Slepian, Ann Elizabeth Bishop.

John and Merline Myril Engle, Ron Voss, Colleen Hedglin, David Diggs, Drew Hudson, Alice Ann Miller, Randall Mullins, Sharon Pavelda, Barbara Potter, Mary Hillas, Charlotte Fardlemann, Paul and Cara Taylor, Nancy and Howard Thurston, Rose Feerick, Kevin Cashman, Jan Sullivan, Stephen Potter, Rick and Kitty Ufford-Chase.

Helen Palmer, Russ Hudson, Don Riso, Suzanne Zuercher, Kathleen Hurley, Theodorre Donson, Marcus Borg, Joan Chittister, Henri Nouwen, Joanna Macy, Rachel Naomi Remen, Rita Nakashima Brock, Jeremy Taylor, Kathleen Fischer, Richard Rohr, Jane Vennard, Rebecca Button Prichard, Morton Kelsey, Thich Nhat Hanh, Ann Weiser Cornell, Jake Empereur, Sandra Maitri, Margaret Guenther, Norveen Vest, Christopher McCauley, Janet Ruffing, Francis Rothluebber.

FLUID FRIENDS

Wendy Bayer, Donna Ambrogi, Elsie Harber, Alicia Sheridan, Gail Duggan, Janet Vandevender and Paul Kittlaus, Ken Dale, Carol Billings and Richard Harris, Gene Boutilier, Mary Atwood, Lois McAfee, Jim and Joann Lamb, Rizek and Alice Abusharr, Pat Patterson, Martha Millett, Carolyn Mason, Monica Matthews.

Steve and Pat Smith, Mary Lindsey, Charleen Krueger, Don and Judy Chatfield, Mary Cooper and Jan Reed, Jeanne Audrey Powers, Lois and Rhodes Thompson, Paul Wood and Karen Vance, Michael Fay, Myron Chapman, Don Bean, Vonn New, Stephen Travis Pope, John Harris, Anthony Manousos, Elaine Emily, Ken Dale, John Denham, Gretchen Butler, Ruah Swennerfelt and Louis Cox.

Jim and Judy Manley, John Pixley, Dawn Finley, Willard Hunter, Eva Fleischner, Henry Rust, Carolyn Francis, Peggy and Bob Wallace, Howard Wurlitzer, Eleanor and David Loeliger, Janet and Ron Evans, Paul Minus, Pat Patterson, Tom and Joan Rawles-Davis.

LIGHT TO THE WORLD

Flora Wuellner, Bill Moremen, David Jamieson, Carmen and Jim Neafsy, Tilden Edwards, Jerry May, Rose Mary Dougherty, Sandra Lommasson, Janice Farrell.

Rosemary Radford Ruether, Marjorie Suchoki, John Cobb, Carol Christ, Parker Palmer, Patricia Loring, Margaret Benefiel, Christin Lore Weber, Joyce Rupp, Elizabeth Nordquist, Sandy Tice, Andy Dreitcer, Frank Rogers, Herb Johnson, Karen Dalton, Lea Appleton, Anne Walker, Trina Armstrong, Jeff Thomas.

Vivian, Sandra, Robin, Janet, Michael, Joy, Maria, Shane and Andrea, Amy, Sue, Jan, Judy, Geoff, Joe, Sunyoung, Sara, Susan, Constance, Lara, Mary, Lynn, Barbara, Debbie, Nancy.

SEEDS OF GOD

Lori Dick, Teri Tompkins, Katie and Erin Dickins, Mark and Mittie Dick, Margo Florea, Ray Favor, Melody Favor, Penelope and Douglas Wyllie, Michael and Kathy Favor, Sarah Nimmo, Andrew and Lauren Favor, Heather, Bridget and Zack Allen, Marty and Neal Sternberg, David and Sharon Favor, Kahlil Nelson, Bud and Carol Nelson, Christina Salvin, Arturo Rossette, Bob and Robbie Wright, Cooper
and Namju Wright, Jim and Sharon Wright, Susi and Jason Wright, Jeremy Wright and Kristi Lombard, Johanna Wright and Gabe Blair, Kirsten Wright and Thom Kasten, Sigrid Wright and Matt Parisi.

SALT OF THE EARTH

Ira Progoff, June Gordon, Tom Duffy, Joanne Hacket Ching, John Progoff, David Duncombe, Cliff Ishigaki, Bert Sheckler, Jan and Jack Arkills, George Conklin, Howard Fuller, Harold and Polly Kurtz, Gabrielle

Chavez, Dave Franzen, Sally and Alex Panasenko, Tom and Durga Fuller, Bonnie Hendricks, Penny Sarvis, Mickey Williamson, Pauline and Jay Siedenberg, Ann Peden, Judith Stone, Kathy Adams, Walter and Traci Hjelt Sullivan, Peter Leech, Jim Anderson, Janet Leslie, Joe Franko, George and Allie Yavorsky, Donna Schaper.

BREAD OF LIFE

Elaine Hill, Roger Ridgway, Jonnie Vance, Glenda Hope, Don and Eunice Stuart, Julien Phillips, Joyce and Jim Harris, Pam Richmond, Carol Saysette, Rich Byrne, Marsha and Dennis Johnson, Susan and Michael Murphy, John Neff, Rod and Lucia Dugliss, Fran and Virginia Geddes, Todd and Marge Evans, Marilyn Hughes, John Stansbury.

FRESH AIR

Pat Hardy, Allen McAfee, Vicky Rumbaugh, Stephen Matchett, Mark Koenig, Shan Cretin, Diana and Doug Couch, Kathleen O'Shea, Lynne Parker, Kenya Williams, Paul Wood, Karen Vance, Gerald Haynes, David Levering, Tanya Moontaro, Constance Waddell.

SABBATH SITES

Feather Falls, Harbin Hot Springs, Wellspring Renewal Center, Sisters of St. Joseph of Peace, Claudia Coville and Pat Maurer home, Quaker Center, Pendle Hill, Dayspring Farm, Alton Collins Retreat Center, The Cedars, Franciscan Renewal Center, Prince of Peace Abbey, St. Andrew's Abbey, La Casa de Maria, Pudge and Chris Hartmire cabin, Lois and Ward McAfee cabin, Mercy Center.

RESOURCES for FURTHER EXPLORATION

INTRODUCTION—A SPIRITUAL GUIDE

Conroy, Maureen, *The Discerning Heart: Discovering a Personal God,* Loyola Press, Chicago, 1993

Empereur, James L., *Spiritual Direction with the Gay Person,* Continuum Publishing, New York, 1999

Fischer, Kathleen, *Women at the Well: Feminist Perspectives on Spiritual Direction,* Paulist Press, New York, 1988

Gratton, Carolyn, The Art of Spiritual Guidance, Crossroads, New York, 1997

Holy Bible, New Revised Standard Version, Thomas Nelson, Inc., Nashville, TN, 1989

Hamilton, Walter, Los Angeles Times, September 22, 2008

Ruffing, Janet K., *Spiritual Direction: Beyond the Beginnings*, Paulist Press, New York, 2000

Shea, John, Stories of God, Thomas More Press, Chicago, 1978

The Sun Magazine, Chapel Hill, NC, August 2008

INVITATION—WHERE ARE YOU?

Colwell, Matthew, *Sabbath Economics: Household Practices*, Church of the Savior, Washington, DC, 2007

Myers, Ched, The *Biblical Vision of Sabbath Economics*, Church of the Savior, Washington, DC, 2001

CORE CONCEPTS—SABBATH ECONOMICS

American Heritage Dictionary: Second College Edition, Houghton Mifflin Company, Boston, 1982

Bacevich, Andrew J., *The Limits of Power: The End of American Exceptionalism,* Metropolitan Boosk, Henry Holt and Company, New York, 2008

Hey, David, *The Nine Dimensions of the Soul: Essence and the Enneagram,* O Books, Washington, DC, 2006

Jerusalem Bible, Reader's Edition, Doubleday, Garden City, NY, 1966

Jung, C.G., (Letters I and II, G.Adler, Princeton, 1975) quoted in Sabrin, Meredith, *The Earth Has a Soul: The Nature Writings of C.G. Jung,* North Atlantic Books, Berkeley, CA 2005

Myers, Ched, Bartimeus Cooperative Ministries Newsletter, PO Box 328, Oak View, CA, August 2008

Myers, Ched, "The Gift Must Always Move: An Interview" in Inward/Outward: A Journal of the Servant Leadership School of the Church of the Savior, Washington, DC, Winter 2002

Myers, Ched, *Who Will Roll Away the Stone? Discipleship Queries for First World Christians,* Orbis Books, Maryknoll, New York, 1997

SABBATH REST—DEPTHS and HEIGHTS

Edwards, Tilden, *Sabbath Time: Understanding and Practice for Contemporary Christians,* Seabury Press, Minneapolis, MN, 1982

Muller, Wayne, *Sabbath: Restoring the Sacred Rhythm of Rest,* Bantam Books, New York, 1999

Schaper, Donna, *Sabbath Sense: A Spiritual Antidote for the Overworked,* Innisfree Press, Philadelphia, PA, 1997

The SUN Magazine, Issue 394, October, 2008, Chapel Hill, NC

Thoreau, Henry David, *Walden,* New American Library, New York, 1960

Underhill, Evelyn, *An Anthology of the Love of God,* Mowbrays, London, 1953

MONEY-LOVE STORIES—A GRANDMOTHER'S PEARLS

Alternatives to Violence Project, California and USA

Altman, Donald, *Meal by Meal: 365 Daily Meditations for Finding Balance Through Mindful Eating*, Inner Ocean Publishers, Makawao, Maui, HI, 2004

Domingues, Joe and Robin, Vicki, *Your Money or Your Life: Transforming Your Relationship with Money and Achieving Financial Independence*, Penguin Books, New York, 1992

Dossey, Larry, *Prayer is Good Medicine*, Harper, SanFrancisco, 1996

Jones, Ellis, *The Better World Shopping Guide*, New Society Publishers, Gabriola Island, BC, Canada, 2006

May, Gerald, Will and Spirit: A Contemplative Psychology, Harper and Row, San Francisco, CA, 1982

Miller, Robert, Editor, The Complete Gospels, Scholars Version, Polebridge Press, Sonoma, CA 1991

Ruether, Rosemary Radford, Sexism and God-Talk: Toward a Feminist Theology, Beacon Press, Boston, 1993

Sarton, May, At Seventy, W.W. Norton, New York, 1987

War Tax Resisters League

QUERIES—HEARING YOUR INNER GUIDE

Cornell, Ann Weiser, The Power of Focusing: A Practical Guide to Emotional Self-Healing, New Harbinger Publications, Oakland, CA, 1996

Faith and Practice: A Guide to the Quaker Discipline in the Experience of Pacific Yearly Meeting of the Religious Society of Friends, 2001

Kidd, Sue Monk, When the Heart Waits , San Francisco: HarperSanFrancisco, 1992

Palmer, Parker, Let Your Life Speak: Listening for the Voice of Vocation, Jossey-Bass, San Francisco, CA, 2000

Stairs, Jean, Listening for the Soul: Pastoral Care and Spiritual Direction, Augsburg Fortress, Minneapolis, 1998

Vennard, Jane, Praying With Body and Soul: A Way to Intimacy With God, Augsburg Fortress, Minneapolis, 1998

Wagner, Nick, Spiritual Direction in Context, Morehouse Publishing, New York, 2006

RELATIONAL WAYS—MAKING LOVE WITH MONEY

Byasse, Jason, "Shopocalypse Now" in Christian Century Magazine, December 11, 2007

Beth's tattoo story in Christian Century Magazine, October 2, 2007

Solnit, Rebecca, "Now Showing: Democracy" in Orion Magazine, March/April 2005

Twist, Lynne, The Soul of Money: Transforming Your Relationship with Money and Life, W.W. Norton and Company, New York, 2003

What Would Jesus Buy? Documentary film directed by Rob Van Alkemade and produced by Morgan Spurlock.

Zaru, Jean, Occupied with Nonviolence: A Palestinian Woman Speaks Out, Fortress Press, Minneapolis, MN, 2008

Zornberg, Avivah Gottlieb, in Ursula King, Women and Spirituality

SCRIPTURE—INVITATION AND PROVOCATION

Brueggemann,Walter, Praying the Psalms, St. Mary's Press, Winona,MN, 1984

Brueggemann, Walter, The Prophetic Imagination, St. Mary's, Winona, MN, 1987

Chittister, Joan, The Psalms: Meditations for Every Day of the Year, Crossroad Press, New York, 1996

Jerusalem Bible, Reader's Edition, Doubleday, Garden City, NY, 1966

Keiser, R.Melvin and Moore, Rosemary, Knowing the Mystery of Life Within: Selected Writings of Isaac Penington in Their Historical and Theological Context, Quaker Books, London, 2005

King, Ursula, Women and Spirituality: Voices of Protest and Promise, Penn State University Press, University Park, PA, 1993

Lewis, Thomas, Amini, Fari and Lannon, Richard. A General Theory of Love, Vintage Books/ Random House, New York, 2000

Mitchell, Stephen, A Book of Psalms Selected and Adapted from the Hebrew, HarperCollins, New York, 1993

New International New Testament and Psalms, Counselor's Version, Zondervan, Grand Rapids, MI, 1968

Patterson, Pat, Doing Theology at Pilgrim Place, Volume 3, Wasteland Press, Shelbyville, KY, 2008

Pagels, Elaine, Beyond Belief: The Secret Gospel of Thomas, Random House, New York, 2003

Swennerfelt, Ruah and Cox, Louis, "An Eleventh Commandment?" in Friends Journal, August, 2007

Wink, Walter, Transforming Bible Study, Abingdon Press, Nashville, 1983

BELOVED COMMUNITIES—COLLECTIVE CONVERSION

Annan, Kent, Beyond Borders Newsletter, Norristown, PA, Fall 2004

Ayres, Ian, "You Bet Your Life" in Los Angeles Times Opinion section, January 27, 2008

Chopra, Deepak, "Metamorphosis" in Resurgence Magazine, Devon, England, No. 241, March/April 2007

Favor, Judith, "Spiritual Practices Selected from Elizabeth Fry's Journals" in Friends Bulletin, March 2007

Fardlemann, Charlotte Lyman, Nudged By the Spirit: Stories of People Responding to the Still, Small Voice of God, Pendle Hill Press, Wallingford, PA, 2001

Novey, Joelle, National Green Pages, Coop-America, Jan-Feb, 2008

Palmer, Parker, A Hidden Wholeness: The Journey Toward an Undivided Life, Jossey-Bass, San Francisco, CA 2004

Wahab, Mollika, "Bangladesh Slums Demand Access to Clean Water" in Choices: The Human Development Magazine of the United Nations Development Programme, March, 2003

SPIRITUAL PRACTICES—DIVING DEEP

Acocelk, Joan, New Yorker Magazine, November 3, 2003

Brown, Patricia D., Paths to Prayer: Finding Your Own Way to the Presence of God, Jossey-Bass, San Francisco, CA, 2003

Burstyn, Ellen quoted in On Turning 50: Celebrating Mid-Life Discoveries, by Cathleen Rountree, HarperCollins, San Francisco, CA, 1993

Cornell, Ann Weiser, The Radical Acceptance of Everything, Calluna Press, Berkeley, CA, 2005

Edwards, Tilden, Living in the Presence: Disciplines for the Spiritual Heart, Harper and Row, New York, 1987

Kisley, Lorraine, The Prayer of Fire: Experiencing The Lord's Prayer, Paraclete Press, Brewster, MA, 2004

Kornfield, Jack, A Path With Heart: A Guide Through the Perils and Promises of Spiritual Life, Bantam Books, New York, 1993

Merrill, Nan, Psalms for Praying: An Invitation to Wholeness, Continuum Press, New York, 2000

Thompson, Marjorie, Soul Feast: An Invitation to the Christian Spiritual Life, Westminster/John Knox Press, 1995

GO FOR THE GOLD—YOUR MONEY MATTERS

Ambler, Rex, Light to Live By: An Exploration in Quaker Spirituality, Quaker Books, London, 2002

Duncan, David James, My Story as Told by Water: Confessions, Druidic Rants, Reflections, Bird-Watchings, Fish-Stalkings, Visions, Songs and Prayers Refracting Light, From Living Raivers, In the Age of the Industrial Dark, Sierra Club Books, San Francisco, 2001

Gary, Tracy and Kohner, Melissa, Inspired Philanthropy: Creating a Giving Plan, Chardon Press, Berkeley, CA, 1998

Howell, Nancy, A Feminist Cosmology: Ecology, Solidarity and Metaphysics, Humanity Books, Amherst, MA, 2000

Lamott, Anne, Plan B: Further Thoughts on Faith, Riverhead Books, NY, 2005

May, Gerald, From Cruelty to Compassion: The Crucible of Personal Transformation, Fetzer Institute Essay Series, No. 2, Spring, 2003

Merton, Thomas, Thoughts in Solitude, Noonday Press/ Farrar, Straus and Giroux, New York, 1952

Ruffing, Janet, Spiritual Direction: Beyond the Beginnings, Paulist Press, New York, 2000

Spretnak, Charlene, The Politics of Women's Spirituality, Anchor/Doubleday, New York, 1982

Steere, Douglas, Together in Solitude, Crossroad Press, New York, 1982

Suchoki, Marjorie, God, Christ, Church: A Practical Guide to Process Theology, Crossroads Press, New York, 1995

Teilhard de Chardin, Pierre, The Divine Milieu, Collins, London, 1957

Williams, Rosemary, A Woman's Book of Money and Spiritual Vision, Innisfree Press, Philadelphia, PA, 2001

ABOUT THE AUTHOR

Judith Favor, M.A., M. Div., is a graduate of Shalem Institute for Spiritual Formation and a member of Spiritual Directors International. She was ordained in the United Church of Christ and served congregations in San Francisco. In 1998 Judith retired to Pilgrim Place and became a member of Claremont Friends Monthly Meeting. She facilitates Alternatives to Violence Project workshops in prisons and spiritual formation groups at Claremont School of Theology and Stillpoint.

Judith enjoys ministries of spiritual guidance, teaching and writing. She delights in community life, partnership with Pete Nelson, and adventures with their four adult children, six remarkable grandchildren and a variety of interesting friends.

Author Photo by Jeanette Miura

LaVergne, TN USA
10 November 2009
163672LV00011B/64/P